A RESTLESS SPIRIT

A
RESTLESS
SPIRIT

by
Don Robertson

PUBLISHED BY CROSS PUBLISHING
NEWPORT, ISLE OF WIGHT

© Don Robertson 1994
Produced & Published by Cross Publishing, Newport, Isle of Wight
Printed in Great Britain by The Bath Press, Bath Avon

ISBN 1 873295 40 5

Front cover photograph: SRN6 Hovercraft, 1965
Back cover painting: 'A Catamaran' by Don Robertson

Contents

List of Illustrations

continued/.....

Trident, Don and John Robertson, drivers, going eastwards to Southsea
    mark of course, 1964

Trident passing Hurst Castle. John Robertson, driver, 1965

The Nab Tower. Before engine failure, 1965

PART THREE - *between pages 136 - 137*

Lord Mountbatten, Governor of the Isle of Wight, about to perform
    the opening ceremony of the Hovertravel route, accompanied by
    Mr and Mrs Robertson and Mr Desmond Norman

Sir Christopher Cockerell, inventor of the hovercraft, with
    Mr John Britten of Britten Norman Aircraft Co.

Vosper Thornycroft VTI en route to Sweden

Mr Peter Atkinson escorts the 2,000,000 passenger to Ryde

AP-188 en route - Portsmouth to Ryde, 1992

Canada, Hudson Bay, 1967. Tony Smith during trials in the
    Arctic. A frozen tree snaps off

Amazon to Carribean expedition. Graham Clarke shoots the
    Maipures rapids on Orinoco River, Venezuela

SRN6 Flatop, Hoverwork conversion. Loading a bulldozer for
    Hopen Island

Skimmer, 1961. Demonstration at Redhill Aerodrome for BBC
    and College of Aeronautical Engineering

Skimmer II, 1962. Testing at home

Pindair Skima at Stokes Bay Solent

Pindair Skima at the Royal Festival Beach in London. Note
    Russian hydrofoil in the background

Griffon 2000 TDX demonstrations in Hong Kong. Destined for
    Yankze River in China

Three Griffon 1000 TD for oil industry support in China. Griffon
    office and workshop

Griffon 2000 TD at Calshot for five craft demonstration on
    Southampton water. Dr Gifford with six engineers

Griffon 2000 TDX. Four craft for Royal Marines at Lock Long.
    Exercise for NATO 1994

Griffon 1000 TD at sea off Castle Point, Cowes

Griffon 1000 TD on River Lea clearing debris

Acknowledgements

Roland Prout who built *Snow Goose* for me and Sir David Cooksey, my crew.

Jeffrey Quill, the Spitfire Test Pilot, who introduced me to Powerboat racing and Peter du Cane of Vosper's who designed *Tramontana* and Dick Wilkins who financed it.

Christopher Bland, Chairman of Hovertravel, for his support of this project and Tony Smith and Graham Clarke, retired Directors of Hovertravel for providing me with accurate information. Susan Darby, who helped me re-write my first book about aviation, 'The Ebb and Flow of Memories' continuing with 'A Restless Spirit'; without her help, perseverance, patience and understanding, I should never have finished it.

Dr Edwin Gifford, my partner, in Griffon.

Cavendish Morton for his kind permission to use his oil painting of *Tramontana*. Beken of Cowes, the Daily Express, Westland and all photographers whose photographs I have used in this book. Also for the staff of Hovertravel, past and present, who have helped me with details of dates, names and places.

Foreword

I was immensely fortunate to share the thrill of developing blue water multihull racing with Don Robertson and then Phil Weld. Each of them, as unfettered amateurs, have contributed so much to the development of this new and incredibly exciting breed of multihull yachting. They were both marvellous skippers who were always willing to respond to new ideas from their crew.

Their imagination, combined with the Royal Western Yacht Club's support for short-handed racing, has led to the development of multihull design and yacht equipment which enables us all to cruise (or race) over long distances with small crews, but in as much safety as is ever possible at sea. It was incredible to see the radical changes achieved in 20 years between the launch of *Snow Goose* and Phil Weld's 1980 'Oscar' triumph in *Moxie* when he was aged 64.

Don Robertson epitomises the spirit of innovation, always seeking new ways to improve the performance of everything he touched. His commitment was total but put over in such a mild mannered and engaging way that no-one could resist trying out his latest ideas, the bulk of which worked because of his consummate engineering skills. He taught me that everything in life could be done better, sometimes by radical changes of tack, sometimes by small incremental changes in design or implementation. That vision has guided my life ever since our sailing days and has led me into exciting technology developments which my venture capital company has financed, apart from challenging the long accepted ways in which the public sector has been managed. As Don learned, challenging the establishment is always frustrating but if you have the determination to succeed it is also very rewarding when your ideas come to be accepted, as his most certainly were.

Sir David Cooksey

Author's Preface

My life, up to 1945, had been filled with the excitement of flying and all the different aspects surrounding aviation but the end of the Second World War, when I was 37 years old, had left me with a sudden change in direction. It was not simply that the life one had been living was different but one's whole philosophy had altered. The transformation from great activity and intense mental tension to a future of domesticity and suburban commuter's routine, was too much for me. I tried to pursue a career in the City and perhaps my decision to give up a good job there was a sign of instability on my part. Peacetime in the armed services did not appeal to me and the future course of aviation seemed to be very uncertain and from previous commercial flying in Canada my experience had taught me to avoid the operating companies.

In the early post war years I had endeavoured, with a partner, to exploit some inventions on magnetic clutches. My partner, Sampietro, was an Italian who had been interned here and at the end of the war had decided to stay, designing the Healey Sports Car in his spare time. Having spent most of my small capital we discovered that the motor industry did not trust an electrical device as a main part of the transmission and those few years, with no job or income, together with the post-war austerity and gloom, passed slowly.

I continued to fly small private aeroplanes but they seemed very tame to me having had the privilege of flying so many 'state of art' military prototypes. Gradually my mind began to think of the sea. My inclination had always been towards speed whether in motorbikes, cars or aeroplanes so why not boats?

I knew that a displacement boat was rigidly limited in the maximum speed it could achieve by its length but a planing boat was not. The thrust necessary to plane however, depends largely on the power of the engine in relation to the total weight or, in a sailing boat, the thrust of the sails. Unfortunately a boat under sail heels over and spills the air out of the sails so why I thought, should I not make a boat which does not heel, leaving the thrust of the sail to increase by the square of the wind speed? From those elementary thoughts I turned to the practical side of trying to prove it. Multihulls were practically unheard of in the UK but to me they seemed to have great potential as did powerboat racing and development of the hovercraft. For me these were all new and I made many new friends because of my involvement. Pioneering new craft is not a great money-making business but it was fun working together and we had our successes.

I feel that I have done less than justice to all those Hovertravel and Hoverwork personnel who went to the ends of the earth on expeditions and oil exploration and who, in the process, were exposed to great dangers, some of them losing their lives. They traversed the wildest country and endured both the cold of the Arctic and the torrid heat of the tropics without recognition, and in this short record I have not been able to do more than point the way to their achievements; there are many stories waiting to be told.

Part One

MULTIHULL

CHAPTER I

A Change of Direction

My first memories of the sea and sailing are of Aldeburgh on the East Suffolk coast in 1920 when I was about 12 years old. My godmother, a great musical friend of my mother with whom she had been to the Royal Academy of Music, had a house there and coincidentally, both women had three sons of roughly the same age; at that time we were 12, 16 and 17. I used to crew with the youngest boy, John, in a Redwing, a 12 foot boat with a simple lug sail. There were about a dozen children who used to race regularly on the River Alde, a tidal river flowing parallel with the sea for 10 miles before discharging into the North Sea.

For many years, especially when I was flying in Canada, I did not go near the sea although I did fly in flying boats as well as float planes, landing on the lakes and rivers on floats. My brother, David who was the second son, was the sailor in our family. He had a very small cabin cruiser which he kept at Burnham-on-Crouch in Essex. Prior to the time I left for Canada he invited our elder brother, Jack, and myself for a weekend's sailing. Having cleared the River Crouch we sailed out past the Buxey Beacon amidst all the sand and mudflats, until we were out of sight of land. Jack was not comfortable in this situation and repeatedly asked David, 'Are you sure it is alright?' When we arrived at West Mersea that evening Jack took the next train back to London!

Fortunately, the collapse in 1950 of my small company which designed clutches, coincided with my old partners in the City asking me to rejoin the family firm in the Stock Exchange. It was a great relief as nearly all my money had gone by then and I had my wife, Ella and daughter, Jane who was eight years old, to support. We were living in a fairly large house in Kingswood in Surrey surrounded by an acre and a half of land on which stood a magnificent oak tree of great age. I had extended the already large garage, converting part of it into a workshop where I was to build several small sailing boats.

In the summer of 1951 I went into partnership with a friend, Tommy Adams who was also on the Stock Exchange, and we decided to order a new boat for racing in the Dragon Class. It was built by Johnny Haas, the Norwegian designer/builder, in Norway before being fitted out by Priors at Burnham. We bought the sails from Ratsey at Cowes on the Isle of Wight and called the completed boat *Carina* which means 'my little love'. She was a lovely, varnished boat which gave us much pleasure but being a keel boat, the river mud was a constant menace as we often ran aground.

We raced her regularly at Aldeburgh with some success and decided to enter her for the annual Duke of Edinburgh Cup Series which was being held at Bembridge that year. Tommy, too busy in the City to get away, left all the planning and sailing to me. A friend of mine, Brian Whinney agreed to come as my crew but although he was an experienced sailor, we had not worked together and of course he hardly knew the boat. I made the mistake of staying at home and flying down to Bembridge Aerodrome every day in my Moth Minor which I kept at Redhill. It was a selfish decision to make but I really enjoyed the flying more than the sailing. Needless to say, against all the country's leading Dragon sailors, we came nowhere.

My experiences of sailing at that time convinced me that I was more interested in the design and development of craft than the mere competition of racing. With the fully equipped workshop at my home I began to concentrate on obtaining more speed by getting away from displacement hulls and designing planing boats.

Since I had returned to working in the City I was able to devote my weekends to building small experimental boats. Using plywood, the first one was a narrow beam sailing canoe with covered-in decking and two permanent outriggers to sit out on. Later, two proper hull-shaped floats were constructed to replace the out-rigger seats, turning it into, what was later to be called, a trimaran. We named her *Fun*.

It became clear to me that to reduce drag the outrigger floats had to be as long as the main hull itself making, in my opinion, the whole boat too heavy while also increasing the wind resistance.

I followed this with a catamaran but, having drawn out the lines for an 18 foot design, on going to the Boat Show, I happened to see, leaning against the wall at the back of Prouts' small stand, a narrow semi-circular hull. I discovered later that the owner of the company, Roland Prout, had competed in the 1948 Olympics in the canoeing event, for which he had made his own mould and hull. He had since made a successful small sailing catamaran and after I had talked with him for a while, I ordered two of his semi-circular hulls and fitted them out at home.

This boat, for which Ella had thought up the name *Snap*, was a great success but at that time there was practically no competition as those interested had their own ideas and there were no agreed rules regarding size. In addition, of course, multihulls were not eligible for conventional classes or for that matter at all welcome! *Snap* was fast on a reach and a tough sea boat but not particularly close winded as she only had a small extension to the bottom of the keel and no dagger board.

As her beam overall was 9' 6", transport by road involved a special trailer which tipped her over on one hull to an angle of 45° in order to keep the trailed width within legal limits. With this special trailer I had mobility enabling me to reach and compete in any competition and meet other enthusiasts.

Having a relatively well proved hull, combined with a standard type of Bermudan rig, I then experimented with a number of different rigs. I was well aware of the greater efficiency of high aspect ratio wings but at that time the multihull sailors were all worried about the risks of capsizing and for that reason I limited the height of the masts.

These thoughts led to a series of experiments including a fully battened mainsail, followed by a rotating wing mast with battened mainsail, automatic jibs on a boom, even a lateen sail. The final effort was twin raked masts side by side rig with fully battened mainsails, rather like a bi-plane, but it had no jibs. This latter rig was very close winded but difficult to tack without getting into 'stays'. It obviously had promise but to handle two jibs when sailing alone, would have been difficult. As tested, the additional weight of the extra masts and booms, together with the lack of lift in the bow from a jib, gave a tendency for the lee bow to bury when reaching in a strong wind but she seemed to be very fast on the wind with little apparent loss of thrust from one sail shadowing another. In fact, as a multihull has little water resistance it is nearly always sailing close-hauled and an efficient rig under these conditions is essential.

In 1953, having sailed *Snap* for two seasons, I decided to build another hull. This was also the year of the 'big flood' when a huge surge of water in the North Sea hit the East Coast. Many lives were lost in the Thames Estuary particularly at Canvey Island where Roland Prout had his yard. Aldeburgh was badly hit when the sea broke through to the river at Slaughden where our sailing club was located, the water flowing in and out for several days at high water. Driving by car into the town we found the sea had reached the forecourt of the old railway station and the whole estuary was a sheet of water with all the marshes covered. There was a considerable exit of population and property on the sea front became very cheap as no insurance company would take the risk and of course mortgages were also unobtainable. I bought for £1,600, a first floor flat on the promenade near the Brudenel Hotel. The owner of the building, seeing the sea and shingle filling the little front garden, had wisely opened the basement doors at front and back and allowed the sea to pour through into King Street. When it had subsided and was tidied up it was a delightful flat with a balcony overlooking the promenade, making an ideal weekend home.

Ella, being a very sociable person, made many friends there and our flat was always full of children running in and out. Ella, who was an Anglo-Argentine, was popular with the local children and while I was out sailing she would gather them together, taking them for rides in the country in our Ford Zephyr convertible.

The new boat, another catamaran, was to have the same overall length and hull centres but each hull was to be some 30% greater radius on the bottom and flattened towards the stern with the intention of making it plane more easily. Construction was to be double diagonal mahogany planks 4 inch wide by $\frac{1}{8}$ inch thick with the mould being made up of a number of frames covered by longitudinal battens. Altogether it was quite an ambitious project for an amateur. However, with Ella to hold things and by making endless visits to the bathroom to soak the planks in hot water, plus thousands of temporary tacks, we eventually finished it. *Freedom*, as she was called, was fitted with a metal mast which at the time, were just coming into use and my friend, Austin Farrer of Seahorse Sails, designed the sails. She was fitted with thin plywood dagger boards covered with glass reinforced plastic coating for strength and rudders of aluminium plate.

The sailing and handling qualities of the new boat were quite different from *Snap*. The increased buoyancy enabled me to carry a heavier crew, even two people, so one had potentially more power for keeping the sails upright. The reduced length/beam ratio of the hulls, however, increased the drag with the result that her top speed was much the same as that of *Snap*; this was a great disappointment although she proved to be a good sea boat, fast in light winds. One undesirable effect of the increased buoyancy was that she lifted a hull more easily which may have been caused partly by the higher mast and a mainsail with an exceptionally big roach. It is difficult to analyse the effects of the two factors, namely height of rig and the decrease of length over beam; one should remember the rule in development which is never to make two alterations at the same time.

I entered her for a race across the Channel from Folkestone to Boulogne, crossing the finishing line second to Ken Pearce in *Endeavour*, but for some reason to do with handicap, I was judged to be the winner. For me the only thing that counts is to actually finish first but the race did give me the satisfaction of knowing I had crossed the Channel in a boat which I had designed and which Ella and I had built ourselves.

CHAPTER II

Snow Goose - Catamaran Cruiser

Sailing and racing fast open boats is a young man's pastime and multihull versions are even faster and wetter than conventional craft. In 1958 when I was 50 years of age I took this into consideration and began thinking of something larger with a cabin which could also accommodate my family. It happened that at that time Roland Prout was also thinking along similar lines and as he had already made some sketches, we compared notes. He had already put his two-man Shearwater Catamaran into production and this was proving most successful and keeping the yard busy.

On comparing our preliminary schemes we found that we had chosen more or less the same hull dimensions of length and beam but a different cabin layout. In the meantime he had already obtained an order for one of his designs but it was to have hulls with hard chines. He then decided to make a mould to enable him to build semi-circular section hulls of wood with double curvature, similar to his Shearwater design. The semi-circular bottom gives the maximum buoyancy for the minimum wetted surface; an important factor.

I ordered a 36 foot boat from Roland to incorporate the new hulls but with a different cabin design and various other features. As a multihull design gets bigger the question of structural strength assumes more importance, particularly so in the case of a catamaran. The type of boat I had in mind was an off-shore catamaran intended to race with other ocean racers with the accommodation being of secondary consideration. It was to be as light as possible with great structural strength to withstand being driven hard but as this was a new concept and design there was no previous experience to go by so we had to start from scratch.

Snow Goose, as she was to be called, was designed basically as three large fore and aft tubes linked together by two main crossbeams and the main central bulkhead. Each hull was of a semi-circular section consisting of 6 layers of 1.8 inch thick mahogany planks, 4 inches wide, laid over a mould alternately fore and aft and across, all glued together so the hulls were $\frac{3}{4}$ inch on the bottom with a 1 inch rubbing strip. Thus the weight of a keel was eliminated and no internal ribs were required. The topsides were of $\frac{3}{8}$ inch marine plywood stretched slightly over some light curved ribs. These topsides were rabbeted into the semi-circular bottoms and glued in.

The bridge deck extended right across the boat from gunwale to gunwale completing the sealing of the two hulls. This together with deep beams located near the bow and stern, stiffened the structure, as did the main cabin, with bolted on perspex windows to complete the third tube. The amidships bulkhead was reinforced to take the heavy download of the mast. We tested the boat for rigidity by measuring the degree of flexing when lifted from the stern of one hull and the tip of the bow of the other side, simulating the type of load when crossing waves at an angle. A 42 foot wooden mast was stepped in a welded metal frame which was located on top of the cabin bulkhead giving some stability to the lower part of the mast but at the same time, permitted the whole mast to go overboard in the event of a capsize and simplified any subsequent salvage operation.

One of the problems in rigging a catamaran is that the forestay fitting inevitably terminates at the forward cross beam, a secondary structure. Any flexibility in the main structure here will consequently allow the forestay to sag. I fitted two strops to minimise this problem, the lower one to a position about a foot above the bow water-line. By attaching each backstay to a transom and by setting up the shrouds slackly, it allowed the tip of the mast to lean slightly to one side or the other when on the wind which makes the windward backstay put more tension on the forestay. Even so the jib must be cut with a slightly inwardly curved luff to allow for sag.

The building of *Snow Goose* was delayed at Prout's Yard at Canvey Island as they were busy building the production Shearwater and were committed to the new order for a 36 foot cruiser, the first relatively large sized multihull to be built in the UK. In the end this proved most helpful to me as the potential owner did not, for some reason, complete his contract and Roland offered this first boat to me while agreeing to buy it back when my own boat, *Snow Goose*, was ready. *Flamingo*, as she was named, was similar in many respects to my boat but lacked the semi-circular hulls, was heavier, and had large cabins.

Flamingo was launched in 1959 and after a shakedown cruise up the East Coast to Aldeburgh, my weekend home base, I took her round the coast to the Solent. She handled normally and sailed well but suffered from lack of visibility forward, the helmsman's view being blocked by the large cabin.

The cancellation of the purchase by *Flamingo*'s original potential owner gave me the opportunity of having a season's sailing in what was then considered to be a large catamaran. *Flamingo* was no beauty and I received the full blast of opinion from the conservative monohull sailors! Pioneering in any field bears the burden of a very human trait, particularly in this country, of being 'anti' any new idea and in general the conservative yachtsmen could see no point in having a multihull. In some ways they were right as it takes generations of craftsmen to refine and simplify the shape of anything, until the lines delight the eye. Sailing ships have evolved since time immemorial but they too were once the result of the calculation of engineers allied to the skill of the craftsmen.

The layout of the cabins in *Flamingo* left a lot to be desired. The evolution of the conventional monohull has gradually been refined over the years but that was not the case with multihulls which had to start again from scratch. At least catamarans do not suffer from having the main cabin being half below the water-line with no all round visibility.

The bunks of *Snow Goose*, six in all, were on the bridge deck and the bottom of the semi-circular hulls were free of ribs or bulkheads so there was nowhere for water to lodge and create dampness and the ventilation was excellent so that she was always dry and free of smells. When sailing short handed, the crew would sleep in the main central cabin within sight and calling distance of the helmsman so as to be instantly available.

As a result of my experience with *Flamingo* we decided, before building *Snow Goose*, to reduce the height of the bridge deck above the water to 18 inches instead of 22 inches. This effectively reduced the weight and lowered the centre of effort of the sails.

Roland Prout had good judgement choosing the size of timber for the cross beams, ribs, rudders and dagger boards. It was not too heavily built but it had extra strength built in where required. The weight on launching was 5500 lbs, which was lighter than all his subsequent boats as he decided to put up the thickness of the topsides from $\frac{3}{8}$ inch to $\frac{5}{8}$ inch. He used galvanised mild steel for chain plates, rudder hinges and the mast fittings, as mild steel is a very predictable material unlike stainless steel. I had each tiller carved with a Goose's head, which was virtually the only concession I made to convention of a nautical nature!

Flamingo was returned to Prout's yard in the late summer of 1959 and was sold almost immediately to someone in Suffolk who was to keep her at Pin Mill near Ipswich. When the new owner, together with his wife and two children, came to collect the boat they were wearing light summer clothing. They had food sufficient for a picnic only, no spare water and no compass. The new owner told Roland Prout that they were just going up the coast, turning left at the mouth of the Thames while keeping land in sight! Needless to say Roland did not let them go alone, insisting on sailing them up himself the next day.

The work on *Snow Goose* was progressing steadily and by the end of the year it had been completed, just in time for a very unusual launch - into the pool at the 1960 Boat Show at Earls Court!

With her 16 foot beam the journey from the yard on a trailer was quite an event, even with a police escort. In those days there was a bridge off Canvey Island with a built in post about 4 foot high right in the middle of the road with only just enough room to clear it in the gap left between the outside of the trailer and the inside of one hull. Having negotiated this hazard they had to cross the adjoining main line railway to Southend with its frequent trains but, having achieved that, the rest of the journey through the heart of the City and the West End was made at a relatively high speed as it was by then 5 am on a Sunday morning.

The boat attracted a great deal of attention and was even the subject of a cartoon by Giles of the Sunday Express. It was an exhausting ten days as probably 1,000 people tramped over *Snow Goose*; this was the first of many occasions when plenty of deck space was an advantage. It was a relief to get her back to Southend where she was craned into the sea at the commercial jetty and we had a proper naming ceremony. Joan and Erica Prout, the wives of Roland and his brother, Francis who was the salesman of the company, cracked two bottles simultaneously on the two bows.

From the early sailing trials in the Thames Estuary it was clear that *Snow Goose* was free of any serious faults. She trimmed well, was high on the water-line, quick going about while the control of the rudders was light and responsive. After a few adjustments had been made back in the yard to fairleads and cleating positions, we set sail early one morning for Aldeburgh on the River Alde.

The entrance to the river is dangerous with shifting sands so we timed our arrival for near high water but I knew the river well having learned to sail there back in the early twenties. It soon became clear to me that the River Alde with its mud and many twists was not the ideal place to keep a relatively large, fast boat.

At the time I had very little off-shore experience myself, although my older brother, David, had often taken me on short cruises round the coast. In his earlier years he was a very experienced sailor crewing for Bobby Somerset in *Jolie Brise* in the first Fastnet Race. He also spent 168 days at sea on route for Australia, as a seaman in the *Olive Bank*, a four-masted square rigger of 3,500 tons without an engine. I felt badly confined in the river and, like my brother, loved the freedom of the open sea, or better still to be out of sight of land. I had been fortunate during the war to fly a number of high altitude fighters and had become aware of the elemental nature of the sky and its wonders. *Snow Goose* was a vessel in which I really began to learn about the sea and its ever changing moods.

A number of young members of the Aldeburgh Sailing Club were keen to help mecrew the new boat including James Ferrier, Richard Riggs and David Cooksey who later became my regular crew. Sailing the boat round to the Solent area for the summer of 1960 we called in at Dover for the night having gone well out to sea round the Kentish Coast in order to avoid all the shallow waters of the Thames Estuary; it can be most disconcerting to run aground when out of sight of land! After several years I knew the route through the Straits of Dover very well but it is a busy area and I always treated it with great respect. One night, between Dungeness and Folkestone I met a single white light coming towards me but I could not make it out until it passed me at a distance of about 200 yards when I identified it as a submarine on the surface.

On another occasion when approaching the Western entrance to Dover Harbour in gathering darkness, the harbour control gave me a red light. I knew there had been a chain across the mouth of the harbour during the war which was to prevent entry but I thought it had been removed, although I was not absolutely certain. There was a rising strong wind forecast and I needed shelter but, fortunately, a few minutes later a ferry entered and making another approach, they gave me a green light, much to my relief.

During that first summer of sailing *Snow Goose* I took many friends and visitors for trips in her. She measured up to my highest expectations so far as performance and handling were concerned but although she had a good cabin on the bridge deck which was much appreciated, the rest of the accommodation was very basic. There were no other multihulls about and I was not eligible for racing under monohull class rules so it was not really possible to stretch her under racing conditions. We used her more as a family boat, making the occasional trip over to Cherbourg, but although the accommodation was just acceptable to my daughter, Jane, and her young friends, it was not entirely satisfactory, so in the early Autumn I took the boat back to Prout's Yard for some modifications.

Sacrificing some of the hull strength by cutting out parts of the bridge deck covering the hulls, we made the two side cabins more accessible while the head room was increased by raising the side decks over the galley and aft bunks. The galley and hanging clothes locker were removed from the aft end of the main cabin and an open sheltered space created by moving the rear cabin bulkhead further forward. These alterations were most satisfactory as they improved the living quarters considerably, providing a little privacy in the two hulls, and by the removal of some plywood decking, actually reducing weight without making any serious reduction in the stiffness of the main hull structure.

The first year's sailing had been without any engine but I bought a 40 hp Johnson outboard and had a permanent metal mounting built on to the aft cross beam. This gave a comfortable cruising speed of 8.5 knots and a petrol consumption of 4.2 nautical miles per gallon in calm water. Some propeller cavitation was noted, particularly in a very short sea, and a 6 inch extension was added which improved matters, but a propeller without a hull above it tends to suck air down and race.

Spark's Boatyard on Hayling Island gave me a mooring for the season and although it dried out at low tide, it was not a problem as with lifting rudders and dagger boards the boat sat comfortably on the mud and, ultimately, was laid up for the winter on the saltings nearby.

CHAPTER III

Learning The Ropes

On returning to Chichester Harbour in the early Spring of 1961 a number of well known yachtsmen came for day sails in *Snow Goose*, including Austin Farrer, the well-known sailmaker generally known as 'Clarence'. He was a good mathematician, aerodynamically knowledgeable and one of the first people to use plastic sailcloth, Terylene I believe, which does not stretch. There were also Jack Knights of the Daily Express, Peter Scott, Chairman of the Royal Yachting Association and Sir Francis Chichester.

On one occasion I met Dr David Lewis who had just returned from one of his epic sails in the Antarctic only to be stranded for some reason in Cherbourg. I gave him a lift back to England making a complement of seven on board as, besides my family and the crew, Sherwood Doulton of Royal Doulton's Fine China Company, was sailing with us. We made the passage at night, across all the shipping lanes in the Channel, and I found the responsibility of having so many on board in such conditions, awesome. I decided never again to take so many passengers but to remember that we were, after all, in a small boat sailing for pleasure.

That same year I was invited to race in the Morgan Cup which ran from Cowes to the Cherbourg CH1 buoy, returning via the Royal Sovereign lightship off Beachy Head. There were four of us due to sail, myself, two crew and Austin Farrer but Sir Francis Chichester was keen to come too so he joined us at Spark's Boatyard. We were not participating as a serious competitor for any prize, but rather as an 'also ran'. Naturally, Sir Francis took over the responsibility for the navigation, checking the compass before departure and making all the preparations; I gave him the starboard hull and cabin.

There was little wind to start with and visibility was only about two miles but we picked up CH1 (the buoy marking the entrance to

Cherbourg Harbour) and as a rising wind cleared the fog early in the morning, we found ourselves surrounded by all the other competitors. The wind freshened in a run all the way to the Royal Sovereign off Beachy Head, where we had to turn for home. We were carrying a genoa as we did not have a spinnaker and I had not realised how much the wind had increased, but on going round the mark sailing close-hauled, we were moving very fast, about 12 knots in a steep sea. Clarence was enjoying himself at the helm when suddenly there was a tremendous crash followed quickly by a head appearing at the starboard hatch. It was Sir Francis announcing that he was standing in a foot of water!

The underside of the curved forward part of the bridge deck had hit a wave and broken away from the front of the starboard hull in the forward area and a squirt of water was coming in each time we hit other waves! It took a minute or so to get the genoa off but as we were reducing speed Sir Francis appeared again, this time handing up a full bucket. "How convenient it is to be sick and bail at the same time", he remarked. Francis Chichester was frequently sea sick but he would simply disregard it; the perfect example of the control of mind over matter.

With the reduction in our speed the bridge decking sprang back into place allowing us to continue but at a much slower pace. The genoa had the effect of pressing the leeward bow deep into the water and buoyancy in the bow was insufficient to lift the boat. On the strength of this experience I ordered from Clarence a yankee of relatively lightweight terylene which transformed the boat as it lifted the bow instead of pressing it down. In fact, it actually helped to lift the whole boat and to get her moving forward in a semi-plane whenever there was an extra heavy puff of wind.

After the race had finished we brought *Snow Goose* into Bembridge Harbour and Roland Prout came over from Canvey Island to help sort out the weakness in the bridge deck where it had parted company with the inside of the starboard hull. By glueing and screwing on a number of additional internal battens and doubling the number of ribs on the curved foredeck, we reduced the unsupported surface to a maximum of about two square feet. Three steel straps were then bolted on to the top of the main cross battens and extended down the inside of the hulls, which had also been reinforced. I had no further trouble being careful not to press the boat too hard under a genoa but *Snow Goose* could have done with a shade more buoyancy in the bow.

In view of the novelty of the boat and the many untried features in the structure and hull design, I decided that it would not be wise to use any special and undeveloped rig. From experience with aircraft I knew that in the development of any new craft one should never incorporate more than one alteration at a time, consequently, the rig and sail plan was based on Royal Ocean Racing Club (RORC) practice and in particular, followed the advice of Captain Illingworth, the well known ocean-racing expert, in his book 'Offshore'.

Because catamarans and other multihulls have no heavy keel, relying on buoyancy for stability and to keep the rig upright, they also have reduced wetted surface with the very narrow hull beam in relation to length, thus escaping the displacement law which effectively limits maximum speed of the conventional monohull sailing boat. Consequently, as the water resistance and wave-making drag is so much lower, the multihull's speed is higher for the same rig, and because the mast stays more upright, its driving power is greatly increased instead of being spilled by heeling as in the conventional monohull.

Both these factors call for a rig which is efficient and close winded, more especially as with the increased forward speed, the boat is nearly always close-hauled and calls for an alert crew who is prepared to shorten or increase sail more frequently.

Sailing in the Solent area gave me a chance to study sailing techniques and to compare *Snow Goose* with other boats. She was clearly much faster through the water but not as close winded as a good racing boat. However, I found that if one 'pinched' we could just hold a parallel course but by far the best action to take was to bear away through their wind shadow and go faster, overtaking by cutting under the stern of the other yacht, allowing us to draw ahead, tacking across their bow. It never pays to 'pinch' a multihull; overtaking on a beam reach, it often pays to go down wind of another boat by bearing away under their stern and then luffing up. The worst point of sailing is dead down-wind when, of course, a multihull has no advantage, but by luffing 25° or so and trimming the sails, it is possible to draw the wind round so that the boat can start reaching and gather speed. At the same time the wind draws ahead of the beam and this procedure, which amounts to tacking down wind, can be continued until there is a lull in the wind when the sails go slack and the boat slows right up. It takes an alert and skillful helmsman to avoid this. I found, when competing against other multihulls, that the slightest mistake made by the helmsman is greatly magnified. A substantial lead in a race round the buoys can be very quickly lost whilst a fortunate choice of course in order to pick up more wind, can retrieve a mistake! Compared with conventional boats, one is more interested in wind strength, whereas tides are of little concern except in light winds.

On taking passengers to Cherbourg and up Channel en route to Canvey Island, I made use of an ex-RAF grid type magnetic compass but it was difficult to find a satisfactory location for it where it could be seen from either the port or starboard tiller. I decided to install an electrical gyro remote reading, ex-aircraft type on the rear cabin bulkhead under the coaming of the cockpit where it could be easily lit and seen while the sender was located in the starboard hull. It was most satisfactory as the indicator needle does not swing but is repositioned every 2 or 3 seconds.

I found that sailing a catamaran at night was difficult. A conventional monohull heels according to the strength of the wind and the helmsman instinctively maintains, so far as possible, a constant angle of heel, luffing a bit in the puffs when the boat heels, but in the case of the multihull the boat just goes faster, during a lull in the wind the boat speed falling off, making the helm feel dead so that it is not obvious whether one should luff or bear away. One loses the continuity and can feel 'lost' as it is possible that the wind direction had changed a bit and with the sails close-hauled and the wind on the beam, the sails are not drawing properly but are stalled.

I ordered a wind speed and direction indicator from Walkers who were, I believe, the first to introduce such a useful instrument for a yacht. This overcame the difficulty and, apart from being able to get a better performance from the boat, it was a great safety factor at night. Modern instruments are far more sophisticated but the idea of sailing by instruments at all at that time was against my own philosophy of having utter simplicity in a sailing boat. However, all my doubts faded when I discovered the advantages and began to appreciate that instruments are essential in obtaining the best performance from a boat.

Although I had owned *Snow Goose* for three years there were still no opportunities to race sea-going catamarans. I still had my small open catamaran and with this craft we were able to participate in a number of races which were on handicap. It was not until 1964, however, that sea-going catamarans were finally accepted as a racing class of their own but in order to achieve that, we owners of suitable sea-going multi-hulls had to organise it ourselves.

During the winter months I would lay up *Snow Goose* in Chichester Harbour at Sparks Boatyard having removed all the internal equipment. She sat on the marshes with all the inner hatches open so that the wind could circulate the air freely. It was a time to overhaul the engine and continue my work in my workshop. During the eleven years I owned *Snow Goose* she never lived indoors and although she was made of marine plywood, she was as sound as a bell. There were, of course, no ribs to trap water at the bottom of the hulls which were moulded of six layers of $\frac{1}{8}$ inch mahogany planks.

CHAPTER IV

Solent Scene

As more multihulls were being built in the sixties I was surprised to find that the majority of these were trimarans. As previously mentioned, my early experiments had been based on a central hull with two outriggers to give lateral stability but some designers were very successful with their trimaran designs, combining great additional sail driving power using a hull with conventional but fine lines. On the whole the established monohull naval architects steered clear of attempting to design multihulls as their reputations had been made elsewhere but those that did usually chose to design trimarans. The talk among yachtsmen was that catamarans could never be made strong enough and wrongly thought that trimarans were more difficult to capsize! Perhaps this is partly true although some have capsized including *Gulf Streamer*, a trimaran owned by an American friend of mine, Phil Weld who capsized in mid-Atlantic. Phil survived by cutting a large hole in the boat's bottom and for four days he was trapped inside the boat managing to stay alive by breathing the air above the water in the cabin. He was picked up by a merchant ship and returned to the United States but the hull was recovered much later by the crew of a Russian ship who took it back to Russia and had it rebuilt. It is also true that catamarans have broken up at sea and have of course been capsized, but at least, in the case of *Snow Goose*, she would always float as the only metal parts on her were such fittings as the rudder hinges and the chain plates.

At the time I am writing there appears to be a swing back to catamarans for all the major races world-wide. With the large sums of money which have been made available, particularly to designers of the French boats, enormous advances have been made and to those of us who endeavoured to prove the feasibility of these fast boats it brings great satisfaction to see these developments proving to be such a success.

I felt, at that time, the late fifties/early sixties, as did the organisers, that multihull participation in the larger off-shore races would create a certain amount of animosity among the regular sailors. Wisely, in my opinion, the Royal Ocean Racing Club (RORC), did not accept the multihulls in these races which were organised by the larger clubs. It is after all, almost a different sport, appealing to younger people.

The Island Sailing Club at Cowes in the Isle of Wight which organised the less serious Round the Island Race, allowed us to sail their course by starting us 15 minutes after their last class had set off. In 1962 about six multihulls competed and with a wind of about Force 5 from the west, we managed to get *Snow Goose* round the course in five hours and fifty minutes. As far as I could discover from the Secretary of the Royal Yacht Squadron it was the fastest time ever but as there was no recognised record for sailing boats, they had kept no records.

The Round the Island Race gave us the opportunity to compare our performance against other yachts which was most interesting as there were, including all the various classes, about 300 yachts competing. Tacking out from Hurst Narrows to the Palm buoy mark off the Needles, with an ebbing tide and against the wind, was a bit hectic with that number of boats about. *Snow Goose* would accelerate rapidly and in order to keep bearing away under the other man's stern, it meant having to take an early decision and on all accounts not to be caught in stays. The whole crew, which numbered five, was exhausted by the time we turned the corner for St Catherine's but we made that leg with the wind on the beam at an average of 12 knots.

By 1964 the multihull owners had got together and, with the help of the Royal Yachting Association, they persuaded BP to sponsor an off-shore race for them. After considerable discussion over rules and safety precautions, we agreed on a course which started at Cowes, went eastwards to the Nab Tower, across the Channel to CH1 (near Cherbourg), then down west to the Wolf Rock Lighthouse between Lands End and the Scilly Isles before turning eastwards again to finish at the breakwater at Plymouth. The Clubs involved kindly agreed to start us then time us in at Plymouth and so the Crystal Trophy, the premier annual event for multihulls, was born.

When the Flag Officers of the Island Sailing Club allowed multihulls to join the Round the Island Race in 1961 I gave a silver bowl as a prize for the first of these craft to cross the finishing line. To me the winner is the boat which goes the fastest and although we did try to introduce some handicap rules, the state of the craft and the design factors influencing them, had not crystalised and there were enormous variations in the boats which consisted of trimarans, catamarans, monohulls with outriggers, and proas. What was embarrassing for me was that for about the first four years I kept on winning the 'Freedom Bowl' as it was called. It became quite a fixture at my home and I missed it when I had to hand it over to Mike McMullen, a very competent sailor against whom I was constantly competing and who reduced the overall time to three hours and fifty minutes in his trimaran, *Three Cheers*. I also presented a prize for the first home in the Crystal Trophy but I was never successful in winning that.

In all these races my friend David Cooksey was my constant crew. At the time he was doing a post graduate course at Oxford and so he was able to get away. He helped greatly in improving the boat in a number of practical ways, was as strong as a horse and an expert on electronics and radio navigation equipment. He would constantly be able to get a good navigational fix from the radio beacons whereas I tended to fumble!

Before the days when the roller reefing for foresails had been redeveloped, it was tough work changing foresails on a fast multihull with no real foredeck, just a cross beam and a net. The violent motion in the bow and constant flying heavy spray, often of icy water, made it a very difficult job especially as it was essential to change the sails frequently. With a boat the size of *Snow Goose*, as soon as the weather hull started to lift off the water we would take a bit of sail off her. Only someone who was keen, strong and fit could possibly do this and David was all those things.

During the sixties many of my weekends were spent pottering round the Solent making an occasional trip to Cherbourg, my crew consisting of young friends of my daughter and local sailors. Ella was not a keen sailor but she liked entertaining on board which she was very good at and *Snow Goose*, with her large deck area and comfortable, dry, warm cabin, was ideal for this. The young ones were banished to the foredeck, forward hatches and cabins, while the 'old' ones occupied the main cabin or remained in the cockpit for liquid refreshment. Here one could shelter in comfort under an extension of the main cabin roof. From Chichester Harbour, a sail round the Nab Tower or to Bembridge for the weekend was about the extent of a family trip. One of the advantages of *Snow Goose* was that with dagger boards and lifting rudders, one could drop a hook and lie on the mud or edge in to a beach for a bathe.

One night in Bembridge Harbour we were all asleep when we heard footsteps. Ella and I leapt up just in time to see a canoe disappearing in the dark with two young men in it. They had gone under the bridge deck between the hulls for a bet, achieving this by lying on their backs in the bottom of the canoe and walking with their feet on the underside of the bridge deck between the hulls! The next night, however, we had a bucket at the ready full of slops and sure enough they came back again. This time Ella was standing by with the bucket and she just happened to throw it overboard at the critical moment, together with some very plain speaking and advice!

We heard afterwards from friends at the Bembridge Sailing Club that two young men had told everyone that there was a bad tempered old so and so on board the catamaran but we never heard footsteps on the bottom of the bridge deck again. We had many friends among the members of the Club because we kept open house on our boat and they would often accompany us on short trips.

A great deal of social activity took place at Cowes during August with parties somewhere every night. The 'trots' or mooring posts in the harbour became so crowded that I used to drop anchor outside in the shallow water off the breakwater. I carried a small hard chine dinghy on board when cruising but often at Cowes one could get a lift from a passing club boat or friend so I was always worried about how everyone was to get back safely on board at night, a danger to be avoided if possible.

One night we went ashore at Sparks Boatyard for dinner at a restaurant on Hayling Island. On returning to the jetty the tide was high leaving about two feet under the wooden walkway. I held the dinghy steady while my three passengers stepped safely into the boat. Unfortunately they failed to hold the boat steady for me which meant that when the tide swept the dinghy under the jetty, I fell in. Fortunately I avoided capsizing the boat and tipping everyone else in the water with me. It was a very dark night and we were lucky to get away with it.

When *Snow Goose* was new and untried we relied on a very conservative cutter rig and sail plan. As she seemed to have adequate stability under varying conditions we decided to extend the height of the wooden mast from 42 feet to 46 feet, together with a new suit of sails. As previously mentioned the genoa had been discarded in favour of a yankee with a high clew and at the same time we had ordered a big spinnaker pole. I have never really felt that a spinnaker was a seamanlike sail because, with it not being set on a wire, it is not always under full control. It is not unusual to see spinnakers snagged up at the top of a mast or twisted round a forestay, a highly dangerous situation on a multihull.

David Cooksey was very keen, however, so we decided to try one. Under Royal Ocean Racing Club Rules the length of the spinnaker pole must not exceed the distance between the forward side of the mast and the forestay deck fitting but catamarans do not have a deck on the centreline forward and as there were no rules for multihulls on this point we decided to go our own way. However, having seen ocean racers more or less out of control as a result of their spinnakers having a narrow foot which tends to cause a rhythmic roll from side to side and finally a Chinese gybe in a following sea, we decided to have a very broad sheeting base to our spinnaker.

A catamaran's two bows (and two sterns) offer the opportunity of a very broad sheeting base when the wind is on the beam and we hoped to be able to make good use of this possibility by using the spinnaker for reaching. I had to admit that in light winds the new sails were very effective and in the open sea with plenty of space, quite safe, as in the event of a strong gust one could turn from reach to a down wind course but when one was in a confined space one felt at risk. With the development of special sails and a larger crew I had little doubt that there was great future potential in this area.

Many experienced sailors have questioned the ability of multihulls to tack satisfactorily. One major difference is that they lack the weight and momentum of a monohull, consequently they must be sailed round relatively quickly, that is to say that in a very strong wind the jib or foresail sheets should not be released until the boat's heading goes through the eye of the wind and then the jib must be sheeted in as soon as possible in order to draw and keep way on.

Meanwhile the mainsheet must be released to allow the fully battened mainsail to feather free without flogging. If the mainsheet is not free it will draw first and the boat will tend to head up into wind, and on applying rudder, all momentum will be killed by the additional drag. In the event of getting into 'stays' like this, the boat will quickly go astern but the head can then be steered round by reversing the helm. In making this manoeuvre the helm or wheel must be held very firmly as a catamaran going astern gains speed quickly and can damage the rudders; a multihull is capable of going nearly as fast backwards as forwards.

The design of rudders presents a difficulty owing to the relatively large variations in speed under different wind conditions. At low boat speed a large area of rudder is required, at high speed a small area is needed. On a close reach at speed it is possible to make such a violent turn that the crew is thrown off their feet, possibly overboard. *Snow Goose* had no skeg in front of the rudders and the rudders themselves were balanced, that is to say, on *Snow Goose* a portion (about two inches) of the rudder's leading edge was ahead of the hinge line and, consequently, control was light on the helm at both low and high speeds.

In the autumn of 1965 I moved *Snow Goose* to Woodnuts Yard in Bembridge. While it was laid up for the winter I decided to make a few alterations as there were rumours that a race was being organised to sail round Britain and, most important, that multihulls were to be eligible to compete against all comers. The rumour proved to be correct and the prestigious Club at Plymouth, The Royal Western Yacht Club of England, was to organise it. They had already organised the Single Handed Transatlantic Race and they had also been involved in the celebrated Fastnet from the start of the Race in about 1926. This was an opportunity not to be missed.

It was about this time that I met Desmond Norman who owned the hangar at the aerodrome in Bembridge and he and John Britten had designed a new twin engined aeroplane, later to be called the Islander. They had both been apprentices with the de Havilland Aircraft Company and Desmond had been in the Royal Air Force. We found we had many interests in common as they not only liked flying, but also sailed and were even developing some hovercraft. In their spare time they ran an aerial crop spraying business overseas and in 1964 we all joined forces to set up a business to operate hovercraft across the Solent.

It was a time of much activity providing us with great fun developing all these different forms of transport. Desmond was a very good salesman travelling all over the world. He told me that he thought there was a market for 1,000 Islanders and to date about 1,300 have been sold. The Islander filled a gap in the market enabling pilots to form small aircraft companies, particularly in the Third World where they acted as a feeder between outlying towns and the international airports.

CHAPTER V

Big Race Preparations

The first Round Britain Race was to start from the Royal Western Yacht Club of England in Plymouth in July 1966. All entries had to be in by June but we did not announce our entry until the last moment as our preparations were delayed and *Snow Goose* was not ready. The Rules of the Race were very simple. We were to sail round Britain and Ireland, in a clockwise direction, including every Island and rock except the Channel Islands and Rockall, with the limitation that the total crew was not to exceed two, and with four mandatory stops of 48 hours which had to be made in each of four ports, Cork, Barra, Lerwick and Harwich. It was a great chance for all the multihull enthusiasts to show what they could do.

The main changes we decided on were first to increase the height of the wooden mast by 4 feet, secondly to reduce the frontal area by lowering the cabin roof by 4 inches and thirdly, to simplify the sail plan from a cutter to a sloop with the intention of reducing the amount of sail handling. The genoa proved a mistake as mentioned previously but it was too late to make further alterations.

The taller mast involved a number of new sails, including a tri-sail, which Austin Farrer of Seahorse produced and also re-rigging including a double forestay and runners. This was done by Harry Spencer, the well known Cowes rigger. The double forestay was not an entire success as we found in practice that the snap shackles were apt to get caught up in those of the second sail and become unhooked. It was interesting to find, on removing the original mast fittings, that the vital steel tongue over the top of the mast, to which the forestay and backstays were attached, was cracking from fatigue and would soon have failed. The West Coast of Ireland and the Scottish Islands are no place to lose a mast and as a result of discovering this crack, I used to make visits to the top of the mast at every port to check all the mast and rigging fittings but the new fitting gave no more trouble.

Although the RORC forbade the use of self-steering gear in conventional monohull yachts, the multihulls which did not come under their jurisdiction, were exempt from this rule. Obviously, in a race of about 1800 nautical miles with only a crew of two, a self-steering gear would be a big help in relieving the helmsman so I ordered and fitted a mechanical version of the type invented by Colonel Hasler, which was the best known and well proven on monohulls. We found that on *Snow Goose* it worked well when close-hauled in a steady wind but in a light wind of varying strengths it would sometimes lose control and allow the ship's heading to make a violent turn into the wind with the sails aback leading to a dangerous stern board and for this reason it was discarded after the race. Years later, when self-steering gear was based, not on wind but by the compass bearing, and electronic rams were used to move the rudders, much more satisfactory results were obtained. In fact the modern self-steering gear, together with roller reefing on the forestay and control of the mainsail from the cockpit, have transformed the crews' work factor; the early days were tough!

The original winches were of the ratchet type which were quick in action but very heavy and with the larger genoa we realised that it would not be possible to sheet it in flat so we fitted two speed geared winches backed by jam cleats. These were an improvement but still heavy for one man. The main sheet had a four part tackle with the tail rope being looped under a standard wooden cleat mounted low down on the rear cross beam. The sheet was not made fast on the cleat as the end was held in a jam cleat which left the rope pointing in an upward loop quickly releasable by the helmsman. I also had a three part tackle which could, when required, be used to pull the end of the boom downwards and outwards to flatten the curvature of the mainsail and prevent the boom from swinging. This extra tackle was not used when inshore tacking but at sea one could set up the whole sail plan taut and aerodynamically it was quite efficient, an essential feature of a multihull.

The normal conventional rig leaves much to be desired in a fast multihull as firstly it requires a great deal of hard work to retrim and this has to be done constantly if the best is to be obtained from the boat. It differs in this respect from a monohull which merely heels over and spills the wind as the wind speed increases.

As the power or thrust of the sail goes up as the square of the wind speed and as the mast stays vertical in a multihull, the driving power generated is very high. Secondly, the rigging wires, halyards and crosstrees create a big air resistance at the higher speed but owing to the higher stresses, cannot be simplified or reduced in number. Thirdly, although the terylene sails can be cut suitably for a given speed, it would be helpful to be able to vary the curvature and reach more easily. All of these features will, no doubt, be available in future years as new materials are developed. I remember when sails were of canvas which had to be dried before stowing and tore to shreds if allowed to flog even for a short time. The aerodynamic side of the problems are already well understood and have been solved. In the meantime we have had to make do with soft sails which do have the major advantage of lightness and, so far as the sails forward of the mast are concerned, are easy to control in an emergency.

When sailing a multihull one is conscious of the fact that it is relatively light and has little momentum to carry it through bigger waves; it must be kept sailing. This is also accentuated by the air resistance of a somewhat bulky hull. As previously mentioned, the bridge deck of *Snow Goose* was as low as possible and I had the cabin top lowered after the second season. It would help to reduce resistance if the front cabin window was sloped at a greater angle and all the corners and hard angles rounded off, similarly where the hull topsides meet the deck. In practice, however, one has to consider the safety of the crew providing adequate handrails and stanchions as at times the motion can be violent due to the exceptional buoyancy and light weight.

One other major alteration was to move the outboard engine from a mounting on the rear cross beam into a box in the middle of the cockpit where the propeller could be slid up and down through an opening in the bridge deck and into the water. It concealed the smaller 18 hp Johnson which I had bought, and kept it dry, but the main purpose was to provide a mounting for a large steering wheel in place of the two tillers. These tillers had the carved head of a goose on them which occasionally caught on one's clothing, ripping a pocket and were slightly dangerous in the event of a fall. The wheel was about 4 feet in diameter mounted on a stub shaft with ball bearings, a sprocket and chain with flexible wire cables took the drive down to bridge deck level and on to a brass slider on a rail across the rear beam via cables. The shortened tillers with the tie rods universally connected, were very free of friction and geared to turn the rudders through the same angle for the same movement of the rim of the wheel as the original tillers. The top cover of the engine box was removable and held in place with a rubber shock cord which could be used to hold a chart or handy for holding a glass steady; a drink instantly available without leaving the helm!

Before leaving the Solent we took the opportunity of doing a careful check by swinging both our gyro compass and the standby magnetic compass, a grid wire ex-RAF type. I always used the North Stourbridge buoy for this as there is plenty of sea room with good sighting points on all points of the compass. To the east to one of the Forts, then clockwise to Ryde Church Spire, Egypt Point, the Calshot Power Station Chimney, Lee Tower and one of the two chimneys of the Portsmouth Power Station. There is nothing like doing the swing yourself to give reassurance and confidence in poor visibility.

Snow Goose was already berthed at Millbay Docks at Plymouth when my wife, Ella and daughter, Jane, drove down with me to the start of the Round Britain Race. The car was useful as we stayed a few nights at a local hotel and both the docks and club were a short distance away.

The Royal Western Yacht Club of England, to give it its full name, had a magnificent position on the waterfront below the Hoe, the celebrated green where Drake finished his game of bowls when the Armada was sighted sailing up the Channel.

In 1966 the original Great Western Railway Docks, sandwiched between the Club and Millbay Docks, had ceased to be used and the boats were being berthed at Millbay Dock which was approached through a lock. The last time I had been to the Great Western Docks had been in 1931 when I arrived on the P & O ship *Comorin*, having spent three years in Western Canada and the Northwest Territories flying mail to the Arctic Regions. At that time the Great Western Docks were a major port for P & O liners which brought mail from the far east. The railway, built especially for this purpose, whisked the mail by fast train directly to London arriving there a day earlier than if it had been off-loaded at Tilbury Dock which is actually nearer to London.

The Secretary and members of the Royal Western Yacht Club went out of their way to make us welcome, allowing us to use their facilities. A retired Naval Captain had visited and made all the arrangements at the four ports of call, Crosshaven, Cork in Ireland, Castle Bay, Barra in the Outer Hebrides, Lerwick in the Shetlands and finally Harwich before returning to finish at the outer breakwater at Plymouth. I anticipated the total journey taking about three or four weeks including the four compulsory stops of forty eight hours in harbours en route.

A steady stream of yachts kept arriving and one had a good chance to meet all the competitors and to walk round the Dock Walls looking at all the strange vessels that had turned up. Scrutineering, to see that every boat met the required safety standards, took a day or two and inevitably some boats were late arriving. There was much last minute activity, not to mention the sound of hammer and saw!

There were sixteen boats in all, ten multihulls and six monohulls. Some of the crews were experienced sailors but the majority were like me, enthusiastic amateurs, with relatively little experience although well aware that the north Shetland Island is only 750 miles from the North Pole!

This was to be the first big seagoing race for which these light boats were eligible and in my opinion the decision to organise such a race was a courageous act on the part of the Flag Officers of the Club and in the event this pioneering spirit proved to be justified. Pioneering is a risky business but then so is the sea itself. As I write, a catamaran has just completed a non-stop journey round the world in under 80 days, a very fine effort.

Ella and David bought our main supply of food for the whole race and I was horrified at the amount and weight while consoling myself with the thought that it would make quite useful moveable ballast. A multihull is quite sensitive to trim particularly when reaching fast or running. While they were occupied with these tasks I checked my charts of which there were a goodly number, including some of the west coast of Norway as, in the event of losing a mast, one was more likely to finish up there with the prevailing winds from the West. There was little information about the harbours we were due to enter but we had to take our own times of our arrival and departure at the designated points which were all at some conspicuous mark at the entrance, such as a lighthouse or breakwater.

There was a large gathering at the final briefing on the morning before the race followed by a reception, mainly for the benefit of the press, particularly the Daily Express and the Sunday Observer who were the joint sponsors. It was a rather exceptional occasion as, although the Crystal Trophy Race was the first all multihull off-shore race, the Round Britain was open to all comers with a very ambitious and tough course.

Each of us were to make many friends from among the other competitors and hangers on so that by the end of the race we knew each other well, having shared the same experiences, and the whole atmosphere was most friendly. At sea, however, it was a different matter, highly competitive but with no elaborate rules to spoil it. We simply had to sign a declaration that every island and rock in the British Isles, except Rockall and the Channel Islands had been left to starboard; it was based on trust.

Some wives followed their husbands around but Ella decided that, as it was impossible to make any satisfactory plans in advance, she and Jane would take a holiday in France. Before they departed, however, a new found friend who owned a large motor boat, agreed to take out Ella, Jane and some friends to see the start.

CHAPTER VI

Outer Hebrides And Muckle Flugga

We set off at 10.30 am on 2 July 1966 in a light south-westerly breeze accompanied by a small fleet of spectators to wish us well. The starting line was in Plymouth Sound with the Committee boat lined up with the Melampus buoy near Drake's Island. Departing through the Western Entrance we could see the Eddystone Lighthouse eight miles to the south, the first turning mark of the course. With upwards of 1,800 miles to go the race was not going to be won by crossing the starting line first, but nevertheless, being human, there was much jockeying for position and being shorthanded as well as crowded by photographers, there was an odd bump or two. Helicopters shadowed the fleet out to the lighthouse but from there on I think we all heaved a sigh of relief as we were able to get down to securing our boats for sea after all the socialising ashore during the previous few days.

By early next morning we had cleared the Bishop Rock and set course for Ireland with an overcast sky and light wind making our progress slow. Crosshaven, our first stop, turned out to be a small village up a creek a couple of miles from the entrance to Cork Harbour. The Commodore of the Royal Munster Yacht Club (still called Royal!) invited all the competitors to dinner in the Club where we spent a very amusing evening. It was all very Irish, very hospitable with much speech-making in which they pulled our legs about our freak craft and telling us we had no right to use their Island as a mark of the course without asking their permission; altogether a good evening.

In 48 hours we were on our way again on the 450 mile stretch to Barra in the Hebrides. One day after leaving Cork and several days after our departure from Plymouth, five of us found ourselves, somewhere off Galway, close together crossing and re-crossing on different tacks just as if we were racing in the Solent. It seemed an extraordinary coincidence and as the wind freshened we all spread out again.

On a journey such as this one learns a great deal about the geography round the coast and also a bit about history. For instance, a large rocky island, Inishtearaght, off the coast, has a prominent, lonely monastery where, I was told, early missionaries had brought Christianity to Ireland.

The deep inlets and bays off the West Coast of Ireland are difficult to recognise from the sea but finally we managed to get a fix at Eagle Island before crossing the Minches to Barra Head, the most southerly of the Hebridean Islands, and a very prominent high, rocky headland. The sailing instructions took us through the Sound of Pabbay, a narrow passage between two islands, to the entrance to Castle Bay which is entered from the east. This was a dangerous piece of water as the huge Atlantic swell was striking the vertical cliffs and the rebounding waves created a very confused sea. With the light wind our sails were not 'drawing', causing *Snow Goose* to pitch and roll violently, making steering difficult. We found the narrow entrance, however, and all was well but it would not have been possible under windy conditions and that route was never used again, all yachts being sent to the east of Barra Head in future races.

Once through the Sound we could see the island off the entrance to Castle Bay but on entering this large inlet we saw *Toria*, Derek Kelsall's trimaran moored near the village; they had beaten us to it.

We were greeted by John McNeil, the skipper of the lifeboat, who showed us where to anchor free of kelp. The large old castle built on a rock and surrounded by water, was near the village and the quay. As we had arrived second, before the main fleet, we were able to obtain a bed for the two nights at the local hotel where we managed to get a hot bath. Fortunately I was able to telephone Ella before she left for her holiday and give her all the news much to her relief, although she had been following our position by ringing up the Club in Plymouth who had been informed of our location because the Royal Air Force had been treating the race as an exercise and had forwarded the information.

The bar of the hotel was packed with reporters, club officials and wives waiting for their menfolk. The influx of so many strangers and the sight of the strange looking boats in such an isolated place was, understandably, quite an event locally. There were a number of unemployed fishermen and no work at all on the island as the herring shoals and fishing fleet had gone elsewhere and the French had taken their lobsters. Friday was obviously dole money day so they descended on the local pub and a good time was had by all, who claimed that there had been nothing like it since the filming of 'Whisky Galore'.

Some enterprising ladies from the village had laid on a Ceilidh, (a Scottish barn dance) which was to take place in a large bare hall with, at one end, a raised stage equipped with an upright piano and many wooden chairs set back against the walls of the building; the concrete floor was lit by two powerful overhead lights. I regret to say that, although there was a small notice to say 'No Drinking', it was disregarded as most of the visitors seemed to have brought a bottle and with no tables or glasses available, many a bottle was passed around. With a pianist and a fidler providing the music, most of the competitors and others from the race attended, all of them in the right, happy spirit, dancing and singing with girls, young and old. It was an extraordinary sight to see so many human beings, most of them complete strangers, totally relaxed and enjoying themselves. Some of our party who had failed to find a partner, gave an impromptu exhibition of solo dancing to much encouragement from the audience.

David and I had a meal at the hotel before leaving the next day on the next leg at about 5.30 pm but soon after departure I began to feel ill. I managed to help in the tacking out through the Sound of Pabbay after which I was violently sick and we decided that it must have been the rhubarb and custard we had eaten for our high tea. There was no turning back, however, as I became cold and found that I could hardly stand. I lay down with a blanket and slept leaving David at the wheel and when I woke up it was early dawn and faintly light.

David had by then, been at the wheel for six hours, unable to leave it because the self-steering gear was not working. He had managed to find his way even though St Kilda had no light. I was feeling a little better so I took over while David made a mug of tea and had a well deserved rest. As we made our way north-westwards the dawn appeared earlier than we had expected and as the islands rise to about 1,300 feet, it was visible at some distance. St Kilda is famous for its birds particularly gannets which literally swarmed around us as if we were intruders.

The warmth of the rising sun was welcome and our spirits revived as we set course for the Flannan Islands, Sula Sgeir, North Rona and the Shetlands. Navigation over this part of the course had to be accurate as none of these turning marks, except the Flannan Islands, had lights and we had to identify each one as we, of course, would have to sign a declaration to say that we had gone outside all the marks. This part of the West Coast has a very limited number of radio beacons but those that are there are very powerful enabling David to obtain reasonable fixes and it happened to be a breezy and clear sunny day so we were able to pick up the various rocks and islands. St Kilda with its towering cliffs straight out of the sea up to 1,300 feet, has an Army detachment concerned with the missile range there but no civilian inhabitants. The other islands are uninhabited and Sula Sgeir is no more than a couple of huge outstanding rocks with no vegetation to be seen.

One feature of all these islands was the extraordinary number and varied kinds of sea birds which nested there. To a layman in these matters it was astonishing to find so much activity and some were even quite aggressive, diving down and mobbing us, one landing on David's head while he was standing at the wheel while another landed on deck and went into the cabin to have a look around. Later we even retrieved a fish from the bow netting still alive and kicking; its colouring was very bright but it was not a flying fish as it had no wings!

At dawn on our twelfth day into the Race, we could see land on the starboard bow, Shetland ahoy! It was cold on deck but I wore gloves which, although wet, retained some warmth and as the sun rose in the north east it was a wonderful sight. There was a big swell from the west and enormous mountains of green water were sliding under our stern quarter with a wind of about Force 5 from due north. *Snow Goose* was in her element tearing along, reaching on a relatively calm surface, going up and down the mountains like a toboggan. Two or three times I saw the speedometer showing 18 knots. In the far distance, right on top of the head of land, was a very bright light which at first neither of us could make out; it looked like a very large balloon. Neither of us knew of its existence and there was no indication on our charts as to what it could be but, as we approached, we could see that it was a man-made structure. It turned out to be a very big radar dome and a vital part of our country's defence system with its ability to pick up the approach of Russian bombers at maximum range and so giving more advanced warning. It was with some relief and intense emotion that we passed Muckle Flugga, the most northerly tip of the British Isles about latitude 61° north and nearer to Bergen than Aberdeen.

This was for us, a turning point and David with his dry sense of humour, shouted at me 'right hand down a bit' as if we were in the local car park, as we turned south and entered the relative shelter of the North Sea under lee of the land to sail to Lerwick, homeward bound. It had been a thrilling sail and set the adrenalin pounding through my veins; it was a moment to remember.

CHAPTER VII

Fast Passage To Harwich

We sailed into Lerwick at about 1 o'clock to be greeted by Derek Kelsall and his crew, Martin Minter-Kemp, who was a Captain in the Army. They had arrived in their yacht, *Toria*, about six hours before us. We moored up alongside the quay with the main inner harbour on the opposite side where I saw a Norwegian flag flying at the flagpole in front of the main building. I asked Sandy Mallace, who was in charge of the race arrangements, what it meant and he announced that I should have known that it was the King of Norway's birthday. It was then that I began to learn a bit about the Island from Mrs Mallace who explained that Lerwick, because of its history, was a cosmopolitan fishing centre. Lerwick was an old town with narrow cobbled streets and a friendly atmosphere with seamen from Denmark, Germany, Norway and Russia calling in there as a refuge and to buy fresh water for their boilers, the Island's chief export at the time. Rather than adhere themselves to Scotland, the local people continued to accept all the nations of northern Europe and Russia who visited there making the atmosphere more like a sophisticated city than a small fishing town. Even the bar in the hotel by the quay had the price of drinks marked up in Kroner. These men, who were real sailors, not summer weather yachtsmen like us, came round and cast their eyes over our boats and with diplomatic politeness did not say much but they must have thought us mad!

Mrs Mallace, whose house was a stone's throw from the quay and on the edge of the water, could not possibly have been kinder in looking after us. She invited us to a meal, took our wet clothes and blankets to dry in the kitchen, sent two boys to collect our battery for recharging and let us use her telephone. I rang Ella who already knew of our arrival, bought some postcards and a sweater for her and a tam-o-shanter for Jane and then had a good long sleep. The next day Mrs Mallace kindly took us for a drive to see something of the Island. It is very bare with no trees but as the Gulf Stream flows that way any snow showers, and they are frequent in winter, rarely settle.

We went to Scalloway, a tiny settlement on the West Coast, with a square shaped castle in a sheltered bay which was reputed to have been the lair for a gang of pirates, who would sail out from there intercepting vessels going round the north of the Shetlands from Germany and Scandinavia en route to the Atlantic. The square rigged ships were not able to sail close to the wind so the English Channel was, with the prevailing south westerly winds, difficult for them and they usually went round by the north.

The Shetland Islands themselves were, I believe, part of the dowry of the Danish Princess when she married the King of Scotland; the Faroe Islands still belong to Denmark but Iceland has its own independence. I think we British acquired a bargain from the dowry with all the oil that has now been found there!

Our forty-eight hour rest was soon over and we left Lerwick lying in second place at about 1.30 pm for the 520 mile leg to Harwich. There was a good wind from the north-west so we made a fast passage without too much hard work. There are plenty of radio beacons down the coast so navigation was easy and we were able to get some sleep. We had agreed, on leaving Plymouth, to keep four hourly watches except for the two hour dog watch which was renamed the 'happy hour'. In fact it was not possible to keep to our watch times as the man off watch had to do the cooking, navigation, log keeping and sail trimming, not to mention sleep which came last on the list. By the time we had reached Cork Harbour on the first leg, we realised that we could not keep regular watches, simply taking the helm for a couple of hours at a time and then heating up something hot for the next helmsman. We never undressed, simply laying down in the cabin wrapping ourselves in a rug, as going fairly fast it was not possible to leave the helm even for an instant except when close hauled on the wind.

We had laid in a supply of tins of Scotch broth as a good compromise between soup and a cooked meal but by the time we reached the Shetlands we were so tired of it neither of us could face it. After Barra it was nothing but mutton stew which we had obtained from the hotel cook as it only needed heating up, and then when we arrived at the hotel in Lerwick, guess what was on the menu? - Mutton!

The next day, with an increasing wind on our starboard quarter, we skimmed along at peak speed. The waves were typical North Sea, short and steep, as opposed to the big long swells of the Atlantic on the opposite side of the Shetlands and, as our bows were plunging deeply into the water, I moved all the movable ballast aft which had the effect of making even better speed. However *Snow Goose* was still plunging badly under pressure from the mainsail and, although the top of the leeward bow went down to the level of the water, the forward cross beam between the two hulls sometimes hit the waves, slowing her violently for a moment. I realised that it was in fact a good safety measure as it was preventing a pitch poling danger and in addition adding to our buoyancy forward.

These were the early days of North Sea oil and gas exploration and David had, with great difficulty, obtained the position of the known oil rigs in the North Sea and it was not long before we came upon one but, although we went within a quarter of a mile, we could see no name on it. There were a number of nasty buoys at about 200 yards radius around it holding the rig in position but this particular rig was not on our chart so either our navigation was out or it was an unmarked rig!

About six hours later we could see another huge rig on the horizon, again not on our chart, but I thought I recognised it as BP's Sea Quest. As we came nearer we could see two strange looking ships, presumably some sort of service vessels, about one and a half miles away. They were not moving so we went close to get the name of the rig.

When about a mile away we suddenly realised that the two ships were, in fact, huge tugs and that there must be cables under the water out of sight connected to the rig which they were towing; quite a hazard to an ignorant yachtsman! To confuse the issue even more they were not going anywhere but the tugs were holding the rig against the tide, presumably while bedding down? After that we gave up trying to navigate from the position of rigs.

To make sure we did not miss the Norfolk coast we made for the Haisbro Lightship which duly came up on the nose. The shallow waters off the coast there have some deeper channels but there are many wartime wrecks just out of sight under the water so we sailed quite closely round the Norfolk coast in the deeper channel. By the time we reached Lowestoft it was dark and the wind, still quite strong, was giving us about 10 to 12 knots. As our course for Harwich was marked by a number of unlit buoys which we could ill afford to hit at that speed, we had to do a great deal of position fixing to keep in the deeper channel. The marks were really for the use of local day fishermen but because I had lived at Aldeburgh I knew that all the bigger coastal steamers took a track further out which is what we ought to have done. However, all was well and we slipped into Harwich Harbour at about 1 am. Unfortunately, having crossed the finishing line at the harbour entrance we had to soldier on up the river to Pin Mill, a long slog with constant tacking when we were already very tired. On going ashore we again were met by Derek Kelsall with his wife and Minter-Kemp, all smiling of course, looking happy and well rested. They knew and we knew that they had the race in the bag.

David's family lived at Aldeburgh, about 25 miles away and as we had 48 hours in harbour they kindly came over, picked us up and took us to their home where we had a good night's sleep and some properly cooked hot food. One really appreciates home comforts on an occasion such as this.

CHAPTER VIII

Last Lap To Plymouth

Our forty eight hour rest was nearly up so we cruised down the river from Pin Mill to Harwich where we picked up someone's vacant mooring to await for the time to depart which was 1.30 am. The midnight weather forecast was of increasing wind and a gale and this, combined with the prospect of the shallow waters of the Thames estuary, would normally have prevented me even considering going to sea. We were in a dilemma, however, because *Toria* had left a few hours before in a light wind and had probably reached the Kentish Coast and the increasing wind would give us a chance to catch her up. We had a close look at the chart and saw that there were a series of marked channels through the sands which would lead to deeper water. As there was also a rising tide we decided not to wait for better weather as it was our last opportunity of getting a lead in the race.

I remembered the words of my brother, David, who had exceptional experience of the sea and sailing, which was never to go to sea unless you are sure of your boat and never depend on others to come to your rescue; in the case of an emergency you must be self-sufficient. He also thought that off-shore racing in sailing boats was a bad training for seamanship because, in the event of a gale, there is a tendency to carry on with too much sail. These thoughts were in my mind as we departed.

We took a series of back bearings on the harbour light but it was rough and as we moved further out the lights of Harwich and of Felixstowe made it difficult to identify the correct light. I began to get confused and anxious, especially as my sight was not good even then and the hand bearing compass was not lit so I had to hold a torch over it to get a reading of sorts. Suddenly I decided to turn in a north easterly direction clear of the shoals and head for the Cork Lightship which I knew, and in any event I could see the flash of its light.

It was a rough windy night but the flood tide was by now helping us and, being close-hauled, we were not tearing too fast through the water. After a time we passed quite close to the lightship and were able to bear away to make a fast safe passage to the Kentish Knock, well clear of all the sand. By now it was getting near dawn and passing the lightship I was quite shaken to see the size of the waves. In a strong wind with a fast running tide over the shallow water the seas were big and the pitch short. *Snow Goose* seemed to be taking it well but we were overtaking the waves which I knew was not wise although it would have been difficult to get the mainsail down with the following wind. As we went over the crest of the waves the rudders sometimes came momentarily clear out of the water which, on at least one occasion, led to her nearly broaching, gathering extra speed as we went down the back of the wave and reached along the trough. However, she came back on course so I then took great trouble to get her straight down the back of each wave as soon as we were over the crest and we had no further trouble. In next to no time the North Foreland came into view and with a smaller tidal stream to kick up the sea we managed to get round to Dover where, although there was a strong wind, the sea was calmer under the lee of the land. It was a rough passage and looking back it is difficult to believe that we did not even wear life-jackets or rope ourselves when moving about the boat.

Our passage down Channel was fast and we were lucky enough to have the help of the tides. We went round the South Foreland and Dover with the last of the flood tide from the North Sea and caught the following ebb tide where the tidal streams converge off Dungeness, down Channel to the west. By evening we were ten miles south of the Isle of Wight and in the middle of Lyme Bay by morning. We made an exceptionally fast 24 hour run but unfortunately my log book was later destroyed in a fire at my home and the record of it was lost.

I had hoped that we might have made up a bit of time on *Toria* which had left Harwich a few hours before us, but at that point our luck ran out when the wind dropped leaving us with a long, slow spinnaker reach to the Start Point. Unfortunately, we had been trying to make the most of a favourable tide by taking a course well clear of the headland but the wind died and finally came in with a light breeze from the north west by which time the tide was against us! Finally, by evening, we crept into Plymouth to be greeted by Terence Shaw, the Captain RN who had organised and planned the Race, and who to my surprise, had Ella with him on board his runabout. They escorted us to a mooring by the Club where we were told that we were second to finish; *Toria* had been there since the early morning!

It had been a great race, taking 20 days in all including 8 days in harbours en route, and *Snow Goose* had exceeded my expectations and the multihulls were proving their capabilities. David and I worked very well as a team without a cross word on the whole trip while his help and strength were invaluable. He was always keen to use the spinnaker, however, and to press on regardless; on the last day alone he made seven changes of sail! I was the cautious one as I also wished to get round the course but I wanted to finish intact.

Most yacht racing tends to stretch tempers to the limit under the stress and excitement of the moment and this race was almost a test of the crews as much as the boats. We came to know our nearest competitors in all the ports of call and were able to compare notes, pull each other's legs and laugh a great deal and yet at sea we gave nothing away. Under these circumstances one makes friends, rather like friendships in wartime, lasting ones.

After about three days when several but not quite all the competitors had reached Plymouth there was a large reception at the Town Hall where we were greeted by the Mayor who distributed the prizes. We collected a very nice silver plaque with a map of the route and a case of Plymouth gin, one of the prizes for the fastest boat on each leg which in our case was the last and it came in handy for the celebration we had on board in Millbay Dock the next evening. Ten of the sixteen starters finished and the first six home were all multihulls, much to the dismay of the traditionalists! We had a good sail back to Bembridge where I decided to keep *Snow Goose* for the rest of the summer. She had completed the race without any damage which, considering she was already six years old, was a great credit to Roland Prout who had built her. He asked me if he could use her name for the class of similar boats which he had decided to produce at his yard on Canvey Island and I, of course, was delighted to agree. It proved to be the forerunner of a range of catamarans including one of ninety feet.

During the years that I had *Snow Goose* I was also involved in many diverse activities both in leisure and business. I used to fly and race a Moth Minor aeroplane, compete in power boat races while managing to engage in other forms of transport on a business level.

With several friends in the Isle of Wight we formed a hovercraft company called Hovertravel Limited which was to operate a public service using SRN6's, built by Westland across the Solent. I was also a Director of the Gosport and Fareham Omnibus Company, part of the

Provincial Traction Group which had started with horse drawn trams in 1880 and went on to own several motor trading companies. This change in direction came about when buses were nationalised but we decided to stay as a private company, gradually concentrating more on cars as the number of bus passengers began to decline and eventually buying the Swain Group, agents for many makes of car including Rolls Royce and Jaguar.

In 1958 I had also accepted an invitation to be an outside Director of Royal Doulton China Company which had five subsidiaries. As the work involved a great deal of travelling I used a Maserati 3500 GT which I had bought secondhand from within the Swain Group, but unfortunately poor sight due to glaucoma put an end to that particular pleasure. As it was necessary to visit Royal Doulton's subsidiaries in the Midlands and as my eye sight deteriorated, Ella and I decided to move from our house in Kingswoood in Surrey to a leased flat in London, not far from Sloane Square so that I could use the railways as transport.

During these years Ella had not been sitting idle either as, having a gift for dealing with children, she joined the National Children's Adoption Association. First this involved visiting prospective parents in the local area of Surrey to see whether their house had suitable accommodation and that there was no undesirable reason for wishing to adopt a child, and then to check on recently adopted children. Later she was on the committee which decided the most suitable parents for those to be adopted which was a very responsible job as it really involved the future life of the child. Later still she ran the Mother and Babies Home in Chelsea where many babies were born and cared for.

My daughter, Jane, meanwhile had finished school, undertaken a secretarial course and obtained a position with a large firm of solicitors in London. Both Ella and Jane liked the sun and the Mediterranean spending several holidays together there but it was during one of Jane's holidays taken with a friend in Malta that she met her future husband. They were married in 1965 on the same day as we started the Hovertravel Service.

Except for the annual Round The Island Race and the Crystal Trophy races, for the next few years we used *Snow Goose* purely for family weekends with the occasional trip to France. During this time I kept her at Bembridge but it is a harbour which dries out at low tide, besides it being a tiresome place to get to from London. Having to take ferries to and from the Isle of Wight, taxis to the yard and then

Fully battened mainsail with automatic jib

Fun trimaran with large Yankee jib

Freedom. Aldeburgh Yacht Club

Freedom. Twin rig

Snap at Cowes, 1957

Cowes Week

SNAP DEFIES GALE TO WIN

OCEAN RACERS GET READY FOR BATTLE

From IAN PROCTOR

COWES, Friday.

It is a somewhat unpopular tradition that a gale should blow for one day of Cowes Week. Tradition has to-day been satisfied. A wind speed of 38 knots was recorded on the other side of the Solent, and all racing in the Royal Yacht Squadron and Cowes Town Regattas was cancelled.

The only race was for Five-o-Fives and Catamarans from the Royal Corinthian Y.C. starting line. None of the Five-o-Fives started, but there were four Catamarans. These exciting twin-hulled craft showed some remarkable bursts of speed of, I would estimate, about 18 knots. The winner was D. Robertson's Snap.

One of these later capsized and completely inverted, causing a problem in salvage which took two motor-boats an hour to solve. The mast broke in the process.

The Royal Ocean Racing Club's 200-mile race down the East Solent to a buoy off Cherbourg and then to Plymouth, was due to start at 6.30 this evening, but has been postponed until to-morrow morning.

FASTNET CLASSIC
World's Toughest

Snap off Chichester Harbour entrance

Francis and Roland Prout, builders. Launch of *Snow Goose* at Southend with wreath of flowers
(Hawaiian custom)

Snow Goose at Earls Court Boat Show, 1960

Snow Goose in 1961 Round the Island Race

Snow Goose in East Solent in Crystal Trophy Race to Plymouth

Start of 1970 Round Britain Race

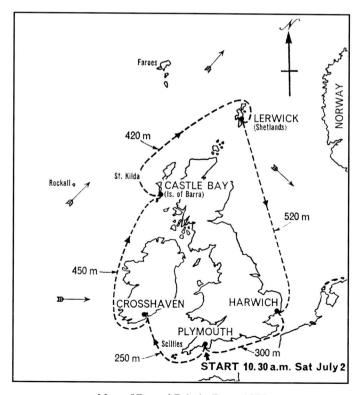

Map of Round Britain Race, 1966

David Cooksey and Don Robertson after finishing second in 1970 Round Britain Race

timing departure and return to match the high tide, all became too much. I decided to move her up Southampton Water to the River Itchen for a couple of years but this was a very commercial port and, as it was quite a long sail to the more open waters of the Solent, I returned her to Bembridge.

David Cooksey borrowed *Snow Goose* one year taking a young party of friends to Normandy and Brittany and another year a friend from Bembridge took her for a weekend. Unfortunately, my friend's wife who was at the helm, had a slight lapse coming out of the harbour and ran her on the rocks on which the Fort is built! Fortunately little damage was done, one dagger board being snapped off. In fact the dagger boards, made of two sheets of $\frac{3}{4}$ inch thick plywood, were on the weak side and in heavy winds I would lift them about one third of their travel in order to reduce the bending movement. They really needed to be redesigned using a more streamlined laminated construction technique.

The year 1969 was a bad year for us as our home in London was burned out by a fire which had started in a flat below us. It was a major fire with the whole building being gutted although fortunately we had been away for the weekend so we had not been at personal risk. It was a great shock to us both, however as we had previously lost everything once before during the Blitz when all our belongings were stored in a warehouse in London which was bombed.

Ella was wonderful, the loss of our home meant a great deal to both of us but we finally pulled ourselves together and moved into another flat nearby. It took months dealing with every sort of problem from deciding on the colour of the new curtains to replacing the silver trophies for which I competed annually. Unfortunately we had to replace them ourselves as we did not have insurance cover; needless to say I hardly sailed at all that year.

Once again David Cooksey, now 29 years of age, came to my rescue by mentioning that the next Round Britain Race was to be in 1970. During the winter of 1969, although I was still at a low ebb, I realised that I had to get fit and having an objective was the only answer. He offered to give *Snow Goose* a complete overhaul and as he was working in the north of England at that time, we decided to do the work at Amble where he would be able to supervise the work.

We had to take *Snow Goose* up to Amble, on the north east coast, very late in the autumn and with the help of another friend, Peter Hole, the three of us set sail on a Friday evening from Dover. It was a cold blustery journey and we reached the Coquet Island at the entrance to Amble Harbour just before dark. It was a tricky approach with which I was not familiar, besides which the wind, which was already strong, was increasing forcing us to make many tacks. We decided, as a precaution, to start the engine but it had not been used for some time and having started it with difficulty, it would only run on one cylinder which was barely sufficient to help us tack let alone push into the mouth of the harbour. I contemplated lying off overnight as it was already nearly dark but we decided to take a chance and finally tied up temporarily alongside an old coal wharf. It was a fortunate decision as during the night it blew up to a full gale and we might otherwise well have finished up in Norway!

After discussing the 1970 race with David we decided two things, firstly to re-rig her as a cutter again with a new fully battened mainsail and a new, bigger light yankee instead of the genoa. Secondly we reduced the weight as much as possible, the most obvious heavy item being the engine which was discarded. We adapted the engine box to carry our mandatory safety equipment which became accessible downwards through a hatch in the bridge deck and upwards through the engine box in the cockpit. A catamaran is stable when capsized but the lower side of the bridge deck remains above the water and the crew, although wet, have a good chance of survival, as proved by Phil Weld in his trimaran.

David Cooksey had joined the company De La Rue on leaving Oxford with a degree in metallurgy. The firm then made Formica laminates and playing cards, not to mention the currency of many nations for which they are famous world-wide. After rapid progress at the London Office he was moved to Tyneside where the firm had one of their manufacturing plants. A friend of his who was employed at Glenrothes near St Andrews in Scotland, and David, were asked to find a buyer for part of Formica, a company which made plastic components but, having failed to do so, they decided to bid for it themselves, acquiring it at a reasonable price. During the next few years they developed it successfully, David becoming a member of the Scottish Economic Council and the Council of the Confederation of British Industry. He was able and ambitious eventually moving south to London where he started a venture capital company. He also became involved in public affairs becoming Chairman of the Public Audit Commission and a Director of the Bank of England. I had retired by then and our lives had taken different paths but I know he was knighted in 1993.

CHAPTER IX

Maximum Effort

With a fresh coat of paint and all the alterations, including a new pair of rudders, *Snow Goose,* now ten years old, was ready for another battering and in June 1970 we made our way down to Plymouth again. To sail Round Britain had fired up the imagination of many new competitors and for the 1970 race there were 25 entries in all, 12 monohulls and 13 multihulls. There were two interesting monohulls, *Ocean Spirit,* a 71 foot ketch with the very experienced crew of Robin Knox Johnson as skipper, crewed by Leslie Williams, and *Slithy Tove,* owned by Michael Pope. She was a 48 foot cutter designed by the owner who made the interesting experiment of going carefully through the handicap rules of the RORC and all the items which carried a penalty he incorporated, ie. narrow beam, low topsides, a tallmast. He reckoned that all the handicapped features under their rules made the boat slower. Although from the results *Slithy Tove* did not do too well (he sprang a leak off Stornaway and had to stop for repairs) he was, nevertheless, lying fourth at Castlebay and was very fast on the wind. I know this as he passed me as we crossed tacks somewhere off the West of Ireland during the night.

We lay in Millbay Dock with all the other boats enjoying a grand reunion of old friends after four years, while each boat was studied by the scrutineers. The briefing was at the Royal Western with the press and photographers present, especially the Daily Express and the Observer who were once again the joint sponsors of the race. Due to start on 4 July the race was given considerable publicity, the little posse of journalists flying on ahead from place to place getting all the stories they wanted over the local bars! As before, Captain Shaw, the hard working Sailing Secretary of the Club, had made all the arrangements for our calls round the coast and we could not possibly have been better looked after.

The Club had laid on a tow for us all to get through the lock gates at Millbay Docks in good time before the start and Plymouth Sound was full of craft of all descriptions. We kept well clear of the line before the start for fear of collision but in the end timed the final run in so that we were in a reasonable position crossing the starting line. Although the wind was light the fleet was well stretched out and by the time we reached the Eddystone we were lying about sixth. After a foggy crossing of the Irish Sea we passed the finishing line at the Lighthouse at the entrance to Cork Harbour early on the second morning in fourth place.

Crosshaven and the Royal Munster Yacht Club were again very hospitable with parties laid on by members and a workboat ready to ferry us about at all hours.

For the next leg to Castlebay on the Island of Barra we were due to leave about 6.30 am. Having left the outboard engine behind to save weight we were an hour late on our starting time because we had about two miles to go to the line with an adverse tide and practically no wind. With 58 nautical miles on the log we had the Fastnet close on our beam at 6.25 pm. By morning the wind had increased to Force 5 to 6 on the beam and we reached Eagle Island, the North West coast of Ireland by 4 am on the 10 July or just under two days sailing.

Eagle Island has a powerful radio beacon and so has Barra Head which rises straight out of the sea to a height of 600 feet. We were glad to have these two position lines as a gale was being forecast in the Malin area. The seas seemed to us, to be very big but not breaking too badly, just mountains of green water sweeping our way. With the wind on our port quarter we were running at more or less maximum speed from time to time seeing 16 to 18 knots.

Everything was going well and seemed too good to be true when suddenly there was a bang followed by a shout from David who was at the helm. One rudder had broken off when *Snow Goose* had made a violent swerve going down the front of a wave. I struggled to get the mainsail off but the battens kept catching on the crosstrees because the boom had swung out on being eased. I took over the helm and David, with his strength and weight, managed to get it down much to my relief. With storm jib only we were making 5 knots but to reduce the force on the remaining rudder we limited the angle of the rudder deflection to 10°, or about 12 inches movement of the rim of the steering wheel. While pitching over the crest of a wave the rudder was almost clear of the water, which allowed the boat's heading to swing across the wind although with a little gentle rudder we still had her in control. In fact, as a safety precaution I also carried a large oar or sweep which could have been used to steer in an emergency.

The narrow entrance to Castlebay was tricky because the wind was dead ahead. I had almost decided to lie off under the lee of the land for a while but then I saw another boat approaching from astern so we pressed ahead. With only one rudder we could afford no mistakes tacking as the rocky shore on either side did not look inviting. After one or two stern boards and by backing the rudder, we managed to squeeze through the entrance into the large sheltered harbour to our great relief. As a result of our slowing down we had slipped from fourth place in Crosshaven to fifth into Castlebay.

While changing sail off Eagle Island I had gone down a forward hatch into the bow to pull out a sailbag. The movement was so violent I had braced myself against the inside of the hull where, to my surprise, I could feel it bending inwards as she plunged deeply into the waves.

On our arrival at Castlebay we were kindly invited on board HMS *Heckla*, a Royal Naval survey vessel, where we were given an excellent lunch and provided me with the opportunity to ask whether they had any good wood aboard for making a repair. So it was that an excellent piece of mahogany just suitable for bracing our bow panels apart, was produced and with a bit of sawing we fitted it ourselves on returning to our boat; a most satisfactory job.

As previously mentioned we had some new rudders made during the winter refit. Fortunately I had brought one of the old ones with us as a spare and we were able to fit that while anchored. John McNeil, skipper of the lifeboat, came out to meet us again in his motor boat and helped us move to a better, safer anchorage. Part of the bay has a lot of kelp and unknowingly we had chosen the worst position near the rather forbidding looking castle where most of the kelp lies. One of the competing boats started to drag her anchor during the night and we all rushed down to help but McNeil was already there dealing with the problem.

Once again the people at Castlebay had laid on a Ceilidh and a large party of us joined the fun. It was a big event for the Island with all these mad strangers suddenly appearing from outer space and shaking up the village. David Cooksey and Robin Knox Johnson had hired two bicycles and following a bet, they had a race to the dance from their hotel a couple of miles away. Robin won but only because David's chain came off. He was quite worried when we left the dance and saw a police car waiting outside; David thought he was going to be pinched for reckless (or perhaps inebriated) riding!

For the 1970 race the course had been altered so that instead of going through the Pabbay Sound which was narrow and rocky, we were sent south round Barra Head which gave us plenty of sea room. When we set sail for Lerwick at 9.14 am on 13 July the forecast was for a westerly wind Force 5 or 6 but having left Barra our indicated wind speed was giving 32 knots from 275° magnetic. As we had to go out and round St Kilda with a big sea running I decided to take shelter for an hour or two under the lee of Mingulay, an uninhabited Island except for some sheep, until the tide changed. At 2.30 pm we set sail again and gave Barra Head a wide berth knowing the sort of confused sea one can get there.

St Kilda is quite a large Island but, except for a small unit from the Army who run the missile range there, it was uninhabited and unlit. It is a great nesting centre for gannets which were very much in evidence as we sailed round the west coast at about 4.00 am to set a course for Sula Sgier. Once set up on the new course we fairly flew and to our joy saw Minetaree ahead with Gerry Boxall at the helm, and we managed to pass her. David was pleased as we had left Castlebay more or less together and he had not approved of my wasting time taking shelter! We estimated that we were now lying fourth with *Ocean Spirit* in the lead followed by *Trumpeter* and *Apache Sundancer*.

Having passed the Flannan Islands, a series of huge bare rocks, David made a note in the log, Wind 32/Knots 34/Rough. It certainly was but it was also a glorious sunny, wild day with the boat very much alive and well. However, the wind moved to a more northerly direction and we had to haul in the sheets to maintain our course.

When we failed to get a sight of Sula Sgier in the deteriorating visibility we altered course 10° to the eastward and it was while David was busy taking a series of RDF bearings that I suddenly saw breaking water ahead over a partially submerged rock which we had come up on completely unexpectedly. We had to leave it to starboard which meant making an emergency tack but it was blowing very hard and the sea was so rough that I had to pick what appeared to be the best moment. *Snow Goose* went round alright although for an anxious moment she lost way before David caught her on the jib as I eased the main and all was well. After 10 minutes or so we tacked again to get back on course and at that moment saw Sula Sgier about 3 miles away on the starboard beam; another very bare looking inhospitable rock!

Our next mark was the most northerly point on the Shetland Islands, Muckle Flugga, 187 miles further on in a north-easterly direction, which meant a hard tough slog on the wind. David and I were wet and the wind was cold and as we had plenty of sea room we lowered the main and hoisted our trisail. With this and a storm jib the boat steered satisfactorily on the automatic steering gear making about 3 knots to windward.

We rigged a blanket across the entrance to the cabin where the doors had been removed, and I lashed our portable gas cooker to the leg of the cabin table so that its heat made the cabin warm and snug. We took a look around every 5 minutes to see that all was well while we were drying our sodden gloves a bit and treating ourselves to some hot scotch broth. Soon our morale began to pick up.

By 11.45 the next morning we managed to get a good RDF fix 59° 34'N, 4° 16'W with the wind still Force 6 to 7. With a backing wind on our beam our speed rose to 8 or 9 knots and at 8 pm we sighted what we thought was Foula at about 18 miles distance. This turned out to be correct and by 5 am next morning we had Muckle Flugga abeam. During the previous evening when our spirits were a bit low, we had looked at each other and said, 'what the hell are we doing here - we've done all this before!' But when we arrived at our turning mark at Muckle Flugga and I gave David the order 'Right hand down a bit', it gave us great satisfaction to have done it again in our faithful old boat. The wind soon eased to Force 4 and with an easy run down to Lerwick David insisted on hoisting the spinnaker. By 8.50 in the morning we had the Outer Skerry Light on the beam and we crossed the finishing line at Lerwick at 12.32 pm, the fourth boat to arrive after *Ocean Spirit*, *Apache Sundancer* and *Trumpeter*.

I had a good look around *Snow Goose* to see if there was any work to be done but could find nothing so we started on the social round! Mrs Mallace's kitchen was again filled with our damp blankets and clothes, our battery was taken away to be recharged as we had, of course, no power. We thought it would be a good idea to hold a party on board so we arranged with the local wine stores to provide the necessary on a sale or return basis. We were moored alongside the main quay so apart from the invited camp followers, friends and visitors, there was a steady stream of locals and real seamen from the fishing fleets of Europe who came to look and pass comment. It was a good evening and at one time there were so many on board that the boat was about six inches down on her waterline marks!

The weather forecast on leaving Lerwick on the 18 July was good, a Force 4 to 5 from the south-west would suit us well on the 484 nautical miles to Lowestoft. We left at 12.33 pm and had been on our course for about an hour when, to our surprise, *Trumpeter*, Phil Weld's trimaran with Bob Harris as crew, who was leading us in the race, appeared from the opposite direction and as we passed within shouting distance we gathered something about a leak. It was bad luck for them as they spent 20 hours back in Lerwick repairing it and it lost them their position lying second to *Ocean Spirit*.

We were making a steady 10 knots while the wind lasted but after 12 hours it eased a bit and we were down to 7 knots. With our Walker Log giving us an accurate figure of distance run and by taking a series of RDF bearings we had no difficulty with navigation. During the first day we were close reaching at about 10 knots as the wind veered to the west but in the evening we saw *Sundancer* ahead of us; we were closing slowly. I steered out to the east of our course to encourage the crew of *Apache Sundancer* to think that we were going to pass their port side but after dark, strictly illegally, turned off our navigation lights and reached across to get out of sight to starboard. In fact we gained speed, missed his stern by about 100 yards and when well clear, resumed our course.

We did not see them again until we met in Lowestoft when they told us that they also had doused their light but they had not seen us pass so our little subterfuge had worked.

During the next night, while I was at the helm, I saw a great many lights ahead which I thought at first, must be an oil rig but getting nearer I realised that it could not be and in fact it was a large fleet of fishing boats. By now I was very tired and with the light wind, sailing was automatic, just keeping the needle of the gyro compass parallel with the grid wire guide lines and for the first time in my life I found myself actually asleep at the helm, standing up! I did not know it was possible.

The first we saw of land was at 9 pm but as it was getting dark we decided to aim for the Haisbro Light Vessel as there are so many wrecks a few miles off the Norfolk coast in the shallower areas. This decision was probably a mistake as there was little wind near the shore and a number of unlit buoys. Also by staying further out we could have approached Lowestoft on a reach instead of a run and made better speed.

We reached the entrance to the harbour at 2.21 am where, to our surprise and joy, the Club motor boat was waiting to tow us to our berth and several members of the Club had waited up most of the night to greet us. We could hardly speak from tiredness and emotion at their kindness and thoughtfulness. We found out later that we had made the fastest time from Lerwick, 2 days, 10 hours, 51 minutes, winning that leg for the 480 nautical miles. There to meet us next morning were an old friend, Pat Wilkins and David's parents who drove us over to their home at Aldeburgh where we had a good rest.

On arrival at Lowestoft I took our battery to a garage for recharging, arranging to pick it up on our return to the boat. I paid for it in advance and duly collected, assuming unwisely, that they had actually done the job. Unfortunately we did not discover that this was not the case until our navigation lights started to get dim off Dover on the next leg. We switched off everything to conserve what was left, only turning on navigation lights when another vessel came in sight, but it meant that we had also lost our gyro compass and had to use a torch for examining charts and for cooking. On this occasion I had broken my own cardinal rule by assuming that a vital shore job had been carried out without checking it personally.

Leaving Lowestoft well before dawn and sailing across the Thames Estuary at 6 or 7 knots we were off North Goodwin Light Vessel by 6 pm passing Dover at 1 o'clock in the morning. We were lucky enough to have carried the tide as far as there and it turned to the west before Folkestone so we again had a favourable tide. All was going well but the wind was veering and the forecast gave a stronger wind from the north-west. It certainly did increase with gusts of 30 to 40 knots from the west and we had to lower our mainsail and hoist our trisail with storm jib only.

It took until 7 pm to get as far as the Nab and with the tide south of the Isle of Wight just turning against us I knew we would make little progress during the night so I decided to take shelter under the lee of the Island, near Shanklin, which I knew had a good anchorage close in under the cliff near Dunnose Head. We lay to our anchor for about four hours and had some hot food and a short sleep before facing what was by then a full Westerly gale in the Channel.

It was a tough day as, although with the tide we were making slow progress, with tide and wind against us we made virtually none, only reaching Anvil Point, the first headland after the Isle of Wight before reaching Portland bill, by 6.30 pm that evening. Swanage was temptingly near and would again provide shelter but, suddenly, the wind strength decreased and veered into a westerly direction. The boat was making progress again with a tide under us and close-hauled, we soon had Portland Bill north of us at a distance of 12 miles.

The last part of our journey was a long drag with light winds of varying direction. I went too far out at Start Point and the wind then died just as the tide swept to the east. By now we were both very tired and listening to the BBC news on the radio we heard that *Apache Sundancer* had capsized but that Mike Butterfield and his crew, Peter Ellison had been rescued; it must have happened while we were taking shelter at Shanklin.

On reaching the western entrance to Plymouth Sound, Ella and David's mother were out there in Terence Shaw's dory to meet us and to tell us that we were the second to finish after *Ocean Spirit*. It was a wonderful moment, good old *Snow Goose*.

Ocean Spirit, a conventional monohull, was in a day and a half before us, gaining a day and seven hours on the last lap from Lowestoft. They had missed the worst of the gale in the Channel and in any case their greater length and weight had favoured them, whereas on the Lerwick leg we had gained 12 hours on their time. Third to arrive was *Trumpeter*, 12 hours behind us but she had been delayed at Lerwick for 20 hours while they made the repairs to their leaking hull. Gerry Boxall in *Minetaree* was a very creditable fourth considering the length overall of their boat was only 30 feet. Of the first six boats to finish five were multihulls. The pundits were saying that the winds favoured the multihulls but they were not there punching into two full gales.

A severe limitation in these races is the rule limiting the total crew to two and I think Robin Knox Johnson and Leslie Williams must have made a superhuman effort to get a big boat like the 71 foot *Ocean Spirit* round so quickly. I was sorry for Mike Butterfield losing *Apache Sundancer* in the Channel especially as they were giving us a very close race and we were all so close to home when it happened. They had gained 9 hours on us between Castlebay and Lerwick and had obviously been trying very hard on the last lap to catch us up.

There were many celebrations and commiserations in Millbay Docks after the race as the fleet was gradually accounted for. The Mayor of Plymouth gave us a reception and speech at the prize-giving in the Town Hall and Phil Weld replied on behalf of the competitors. As an American he told us that, in the distant past, his relations had come from Cornwall and that he was honoured to be asked to speak. He was certainly the most popular among the competitors and a most enthusiastic multihull sailor.

David and I were presented with the prize for the first multihull to finish, but of course we were second in the race itself just as we had been in the first race in 1966.

David went on to sail in the 1974 and 1978 races with Phil Weld coming third in each race.

CHAPTER X

Reflections

The modifications which we had made to *Snow Goose* had certainly made her faster and we were, of course, delighted at our success at being second but for me there was greater satisfaction from actually finishing while, at the same time, having the opportunity to demonstrate the capabilities of multihulls. After many early experiments, and knowing of the past history of the Polynesian craft in the Pacific, I felt that the unballasted sailing boat had a great potential which had not been realised by the conventional yachtsman.

I appreciate the beauty of the monohull sailing boat whose lines and construction have been developed over hundreds of years but nowadays we have so many new materials that designers have every opportunity to experiment with the greater strength and lightweight materials which have not yet been fully exploited.

I believe that David Cooksey would probably have done better than I because he is a true racing man. My own caution was perhaps the price of age but I know the sea and I am very aware that accidents do happen; the important thing was to finish. I also know how important it is to keep a little of one's strength in reserve for an emergency and not to go on to the point of exhaustion.

In the second race we had left our outboard engine behind. I remember my brother David, who really was a sailor, once telling me that to sail without an engine was true sailing because it makes one think ahead. He also advised me always to treat the sea with respect. My own background was based on a love of engines whether they were in motorbikes, cars, aeroplanes, or even power boats but the psychology of sailing should not include an engine to get you home! Admittedly it is different if you only sail in the Solent at weekends and your crew have to get back to catch a train in order to be at work on Monday, but having no engine gave me a great feeling of satisfaction; at least we had circled our Island home making use of the elements alone.

Although a boat is an inanimate object it is strange how it seems to take on a character. After ten years I knew *Snow Goose* and what she could do, both in performance and handling. I was familiar with how she would respond in any normal circumstances but by the end of the 1970 race it had become more than that. She felt like an old worn coat or pair of shoes, comfortable and reassuring. After 3 weeks of racing and living on board, the sea itself almost becomes a friend and a combination of boat and sea merge and become one. I had never been conscious of it before but I have no doubt that many sailors must have experienced this sensation. Up to that time I had always envisaged the boat as a mechanical structure embodying well known technical features but it now, somehow, took on a different role.

At 62 my eyes were poor and shortly afterwards the doctors found that I had glaucoma as well as high blood pressure. It was then I knew that I had sailed my last Round Britain Race. However, David and I had learned a thing or two and after many discussions I decided to design a new and bigger boat.

There were two main factors which badly needed improvement or even an entirely fresh approach. One was a method of self-steering which was not just dependent on the wind and its relationship to the sails, but one which responded to the desired heading determined by a magnetic gyro stabilised compass. Not being able to leave the helm for an instant meant that the off-duty crew was constantly being called to trim the sails. The other requirement was to be able to increase or decrease the sail areas from the cockpit with the minimum effort. The roller reefing gear on the forestay dates from Edwardian days but it had dropped out of use. A well cut sail will always set better than one which has the luff rolled up.

My friend, Phil Weld, brought over from the United States, an up to date American version on his trimaran *Gulf Streamer*. The foresail, with a beaded luff, was fed into a streamlined metal extrusion through a groove and the area controlled by turning it with a pulley and cable in the cockpit. In a rather similar manner his new boat in 1979 called *Moxie* had a vertical roller reefing device just aft of the main mast so that the mainsail area was reefed vertically, not horizontally, as is usual. The experts criticised this as being very inefficient with the small air gap between the mast and the roller but in fact he won the single handed Transatlantic race with it! All his sails could be controlled without leaving the cockpit.

During the 1972 Transatlantic Race, Phil went up to the top of the mast while in mid-Atlantic, for what reason I do not know. While he was up there the main halyard had slipped between the slot of the sheeve and the mast where it had jammed. Phil, who had hauled himself up by the spinnaker halyard, was unable to release anything, himself included. He remained there, marooned, for about an hour before he decided he had to try and get back down to the deck. It was a very frightening experience.

Phil kindly invited me to crew for him in *Rogue Wave* in the Round the Island Race in 1976. There was a strong northerly wind and on the reach from Bembridge Ledge to the Forts we touched 25 knots. She had even been doing 14 knots when close-hauled on the wind on the way from St Catherine's Point to Bembridge Ledge. Beken, the famous photographer from Cowes, came out to take some photographs near the Bembridge Fort and could not keep up in his power boat! It was interesting to note that with the strong wind at right angles to our course everything was hauled right in taut, ie. close-hauled. One was conscious of the whole boat and rig being under enormous strain with the leeward outrigger throwing up a big bow wave and a huge rooster tail astern; it was no time to sit and read a newspaper in the cabin!

Having sketched out our new design incorporating all our ideas, a 72 foot catamaran with three main cross beams and a small pod in the centre as a cabin, we consulted Souters of Cowes about costs. They quickly gave us a preliminary figure of cost because they were keen to build it but they also made a beautiful 1/20th scale model which went on to their stand at the 1972 Boat Show at Earls Court. Having several years previously, made some experiments with a side by side bi-plane type, twin rig on an 18 foot catamaran, I was keen to rig the new boat similarly by mounting two tall cutter rigs side by side with a big gap between the mainsails. On a bi-plane type of aeroplane the gap between the wings needs to be at least one and a half times the chord of the wing. We could not quite get as big a gap as this but up to about 100 miles per hour a bi-plane is quite an efficient aeroplane. I believe, on a catamaran in a heavy wind, by lowering the lee rig completely, the windward rig would not need to be reefed and would be efficient, with the whole arrangement performing like a Polynesian proa.

We tried to get sponsorship but it was not a good time financially and combined with the fact that David was just starting a new company in Scotland which meant that he did not have much time, the idea was dropped, much to my regret. During the time *Snow Goose* was laid up at Groves and Gutteridge in Cowes I decided that my sailing days were over and I put her on the market. Eventually John Hart, the senior sailing instructor at the Cowes Sailing School bought her, taking her up to Morecombe Bay on the north west coast near his new job on Lake Windermere. I was glad to see her appear for the third time at Plymouth for the start of the Round Britain Race in 1974 by which time she was getting badly dated. However, she finished fifteenth which was not bad for a fourteen year old boat!

I have often told my friends that buying a yacht is the quickest way of getting rid of your money but for me *Snow Goose* was not only good value in a financial sense (she only cost about £1,900 in 1959 plus another thousand to equip) but she became a way of life enabling me to see a different world; new people, new friends who had a spirit of pioneering a new venture and learning about the sea. We are a maritime race and yet most people hardly know our coastal waters or the beauties of our Islands let alone their often violent and historic past. The two Round Britain Races opened my eyes to the wonders of the elements and the open sea, not to mention so many strange sea birds.

Snow Goose bore us safely and swiftly to our destinations until, through the years, I came to know her like an old friend that I could trust. She introduced us to the sea with all its infinite variety of mood from gentleness, calm, oily smoothness to violent rage. I have always had the greatest respect for the sea and its dangers and one must never disregard them. When things go wrong, difficulties are compounded and it is wise to retain, if possible, one's strength and never get exhausted in order to have some reserve strength to deal with these occasions. Under wet and cold conditions the upkeep of morale of the crew is vital when hot food is more sustaining than alcohol although the latter should not be left behind as half the pleasure is the social side reminiscing in harbour!

To be at sea in a gale in a small boat is to realise how infinitely powerful are the elements and how puny is man's strength. Yet with a well found and, in our case, unsinkable boat, one begins to feel at one with the boat and at ease, almost part of the sea.

The two Prout brothers, Francis and Roland, have every reason to feel proud of their work in building *Snow Goose*. She was light and buoyant responding instantly and sometimes violently to the upheavals of a storm but, like every vessel in rough conditions, she needed the gentle touch, anticipation and watchfulness for any hint of undue stress.

As with the pilot of an aeroplane who cannot relax the tension until he has landed safely on good old mother earth, so the skipper in charge of a boat is under the same pressure until he is safely berthed in harbour. Considering the novelty and unknown forces involved in building an entirely new type of sailing vessel I always felt that I had a very sound and strong boat which would not let me down. I was greatly honoured when the Prout brothers asked if they could use her name for the Class which then went into production.

Part Two

POWERBOAT
RACING

CHAPTER XI

A Lucky Break

My early years had been dominated by my love of aircraft but since leaving the Stock Exchange in 1955 my training and age counted against my finding a job in aviation. In 1959, however, Christopher Cockerell (now Sir) invented the hovercraft, a fascinating development which brings, in many ways, aviation and the sea together; both are moving elemental forces outside man's control. The theme of this book is, of course, the sea and I had already tried to apply some of my background knowledge of aviation to making faster sailing boats. Having a workshop at home and, having made a number of racing catamarans, the idea of a home-made hovercraft appealed to me. *Snow Goose* had recently been completed and was berthed at Canvey Island so the hovercraft would keep me busy in my spare time at home.

The original SRN1, based on Christopher Cockerell's design and built by Westland, the aircraft company at Cowes, was the first to be publicly demonstrated using an aeroplane engine driving a conventional, wooden propeller with the axis mounted vertically in a duct, for both lift and thrust. Having been involved during the war with the first jets which had centrifugal fans, it seemed natural to me to use one in a hovercraft. The centrifugal fan, when turning, does not allow the air to flow backwards which to my mind was the key to future designs and in fact it proved to be the forerunner of all later designs of hovercraft for providing air for lift.

It was while I was experimenting with this in the spring of 1962 that I had an accident managing to cut off the tips of all the fingers of my right hand in the fan. My wife, Ella, who understandably was a bit shaken, drove me to our nearest hospital at Epsom but being a Saturday afternoon they were unable to cope and, having given me a shot of something, they sent me on to Roehampton in an ambulance.

Within half an hour they had me on the operating table and tidied up the ends of my fingers. The actual tips were missing, spread over my lawn at home or caught up underneath the craft but fortunately my thumb was untouched and so I was still able to grip things.

On regaining consciousness Ella gave me a letter which had arrived from Jeffrey Quill, my old friend from Supermarine days, asking me to be his number two driver in the Cowes to Torquay Power Boat Race which was to take place in September of that year. It cheered me up a great deal as I had been wondering what activities I should have to give up. In fact I was home in less than a week and within a month I was contemplating how to tackle the finishing pieces to the hovercraft. Jeffrey's invitation gave me an incentive to get fit again quickly and by an extraordinary co-incidence he told me that the powerboat was being built for an old partner of mine in the City, Dick Wilkins.

Dick was a friend of Tommy Sopwith whose father was the pioneer airman. Sopwith had won the 1961 Cowes to Torquay race with a boat built by Fairey Marine on the Hamble River. Dick used to race cars, usually Alfas, at Brooklands in the pre-war days and had jokingly bet Tommy £5 that he could beat him to Torquay. He then went secretly to Vospers, the Portsmouth boatbuilders and commissioned Peter du Cane, the famous designer, to build him a boat which at all costs had to win the coming race!

Peter, who had designed the wartime MTB's and post-war fast gas turbine engined Patrol Boats for the Royal Navy, immediately set to work on the design. This was ultimately named *Tramontana*, which had been the name of an old sailing boat of Dick's and is, of course, the name of the northern wind from the mountains in the Mediterranean area. She was just under 40 feet long, the rule limit, and, as was to be expected, followed previous Vosper practice of a warped vee bottom, a buoyant bow and was of great strength, built in wood.

The engines were to be two Italian CRM 18 cylinder petrol engines each with three banks of six cylinders, on a broad arrow type crankcase. These engines were well known to Vospers as they had used them in the pre-war MTB's (motor torpedo boats) and the two engines for *Tramontana* were unused spares. Originally these engines were designed and built by Isotta Fraschini Aeroplane Engines and were used in the big Savoia Maschetti flying boats, a squadron of which flew across the Atlantic under the command of General Balbo in about 1930, the name being changed to CRM when Mussolini nationalised the Company. During the War the Royal Air Force used the word Balbo to denote any very large formation of aircraft; it almost became another word for 'maximum effort'.

The cylinder capacity was 57 litres per engine and each delivered 1150 hp at 2000 rpm. Vospers make their own 'V' drive gearbox to reverse the transmission line to the propeller with the engine in the stern but, for this application, instead of gearing down the propeller, the gearbox was inverted which speeded up the output shaft to drive a super cavitating propeller. A compressed air bottle, charged by a small two-stroke engined pump with distributors on the main engines, together with a hand operated booster ignition magneto, were used for starting up this somewhat formidable piece of machinery. The routine rigidly adhered to was for the covers over the machinery space to be removed and the ventilation fans energised. After 15 minutes the whole crew would go ashore except the engineer who would take up his position prime the fuel system, apply a number of strokes to the doping pump and, having set the throttles, turn the handle of the booster mag, at the same time releasing the compressed air. This was followed by a loud bang as the engine turned and burst into life.

There were no silencers but the surplus cooling salt water from the two heat exchangers was fed to the two large pipes bulging out along each side of the stern quarter in order to cool the exhaust pipe and quieten the noise.

Cowes, is the hub of the yacht racing fraternity in the Solent area and the centre of activity, particularly in August when the now famous Cowes Week takes place. Keen deep water sailors are there throughout the year but during this time the town is packed with visitors and the whole Island becomes alive. The Royal Yacht is anchored in the 'Roads' and the sense of fashion is heightened as the social round descends upon the area. Parties, bars, bistros and expensive restaurants provide lively entertainment with dancing every night and on the Friday night there is a grand firework display; in other words, it is fun. The locals often rent their houses to visitors for the week, or month, using the proceeds to have a good holiday elsewhere.

My sailing club in Cowes was the popular Island Sailing Club for the serious sailor while the other clubs seemed to cater for all the different types from the Noble Lord to the Local Plumber. When Jeffrey Quill asked me to drive *Tramontana* with him in the International Cowes to Torquay race, yet another type of character appeared on the scene. The local clubs had tactfully, more or less, finished their sailing races by September as the new and noisy influx appeared.

In 1962 when the second race was scheduled, my own experience of power boat racing was nil but Jeffrey and I had both been test pilots and were accustomed to handling expensive pieces of powerful machinery and Peter du Cane of Vosper Thornycroft, who had been asked to find a driver by the boat's owner, Dick Wilkins, did not want a young man. Big powerboats are expensive to build and very costly to run and the whole programme was set up on a lavish scale. In the early years the race was entered largely by rich amateurs as the Le Mans 24 hour car race had also been.

Soon after the second Cowes to Torquay Race the American car manufacturers, with their big V-8 engines, came over causing the rules to be changed the next year limiting the engine size to 16 litres for petrol engines or 32 litres for diesel. This was because the British competitors did not have access to large petrol driven engines making the race unfair to us. There was no market in the UK for big, and indeed dangerous, petrol engined boats which tended to blow up when fumes in the bilges ignited from a spark from a starter motor switch. Following these changes the powerboat became highly professional and outside the range of the amateur.

For publicity purposes the moving pictures taken from helicopters were highly spectacular and the participating boats were therefore covered with sponsorship and advertising across the deck area; not exactly Cowes' style! The September 1962 event was promoted by Sir Max Aitken, the owner of the Daily Express, who was a keen sailor and much liked in Cowes where he had a house on the harbour waterfront. It brought many visitors and money to the town and although the general atmosphere was different, it only lasted about a week before it all disappeared.

The rules in the UK were intended to improve the qualities of the fast cabin cruiser and its sea going capabilities. However, there were very few rules for the race although the craft had to be no more than 40 feet overall and have a simple cabin with bunks and a minimum in cooking facilities; there was no mention of engine size at that time. In the United States, powerboat racing was quite common and they had developed boats, without cabins, specifically for racing and with the most powerful petrol engines available. In order to adhere to the UK rules, they incorporated into their designs, a 'space', in which one could barely crouch and which could be loosely described as a 'cabin'.

Well before September my fingers had healed completely and with Ella's agreement that I was fully fit to drive, I entered the race.

During May, Jeffrey and I drove down to Vosper's Yard at Portchester. Peter du Cane had a general arrangement drawing of the new boat on his drawing board and we went over various aspects of the design. Neither of us had any real experience of racing powerboats but Jeffrey, with his background of the development of the Spitfire was, undoubtedly, the greatest expert in the country on the development and handling of high speed aircraft and his knowledge would be invaluable. After half an hour's discussion Peter surprised us by saying 'Come and have a look at the mock up of the cockpit and cabin'. The crew were to be four, Lovegrove, engineer, ex-Navy and Sam Hutchins, shipwright, who was a real seaman which was very reassuring. Lovegrove was a hero of the St Nazaire raid when the Navy blew up the lock gates of the German submarine base. He had picked up his commanding officer from the water as they escaped in an MTB. I was to relieve Jeffrey over part of the estimated 5 hour race. Later Commander Dick Michel of the Decca Navigator Company joined us as it was decided to install Decca Equipment before the race in case of fog.

The mock up and layout of the controls was arranged for three seats with the skipper and driver on the port side. We suggested a raised central seat to give a better all round view and a more dominating position for the driver. Instead of the throttle controls suggested, Jeffrey, who still worked for Vickers Aviation Company at Weybridge, offered to try and obtain a VC-10 multi-engined aircraft style throttle control box. This he did and we found it a great asset when one had constantly to move the two throttle levers on the nine dual carburettors of each engine. Within less than an hour the mock up had been rebuilt and we were able to finalise the revision, including the position of the throttle bank and instruments.

I was surprised to see the very close spacing of the lightweight ribs of the hull. Four main built-up box beams supported the engines but, with a fast boat in a rough sea, Peter told me that the sides of the boat tend to bend outwards or 'lozenge', and rib failures were all too common.

He was also a believer in plenty of buoyancy forward; going fast in a following sea can lead to trouble from diving deep into the back of a wave. The gap between the two main beams under the floor boards was used to feed cold ventilation and combustion air from a scoop on the foredeck to the machinery space. The bow compartment also contained a ballast tank for forward trimming in a heavy sea. This was filled from a retractable forward facing scoop under the hull and when full, the overflow was fed upwards on the foredeck, giving a very effective signal to the driver by projecting a fountain of spray upwards.

On a second visit the boat was nearly finished except for the completion of the installation of the engines. Nearly all engine failures are caused by minor mistakes in installation and this was a strong point of Vospers with their vast experience; their Mr Street had been doing this for the previous thirty years. To avoid complication the ahead/astern controls of the two gearboxes were installed in the machinery space under the controls of the engineer in charge who was also in sight of the driver giving signals by hand. Fast boats with fixed pitch propellers are difficult to manoeuvre as even at idling rpm with the clutches engaged, the minimum speed is high. In *Tramontana*'s case it was about 8 knots. Making a 'U' turn in a narrow crowded harbour such as Poole, was not popular with other moored boats!

Two fuel tanks with a total capacity of 750 gallons of 100 octane petrol, were mounted to port and starboard of the cockpit. These fed by gravity to a single service tank mounted low down in the hull and thence to a number of fuel pumps, filters and cocks under the supervision of the engineer. This layout, by pressurising the system, avoided any air locks. The main fresh water cooling water, after passing through a heat exchanger, had bleed pipes which led from the highest point on each pipe throughout the engine to avoid trapping air or steam.

A multiplicity of these pipes was led to a plastic transparent tank at the highest point on either side of the cockpit where they were visible to the driver and vented to atmosphere. This elaborate installation was the result of many years bitter experience from air locks in the fuel line and local steam traps causing overheating.

CHAPTER XII

Fitting Out And Sea Trials

Although the race was not to be run until September, we were anxious to carry out sea trials in good time and to 'work-up' by making at least one long cruise. The Manager, Nigel Tunnicliffe, an ex-guards officer whose wife, Diana, was the daughter of Peter du Cane, was a very 'press on' type and just the man to give leadership and inspiration to his team. The time between taking out the engines from their boxes until our first sea trials, was only three weeks. Nigel would sit on the gunwhale, legs dangling in the machinery space, directing the operation of half a dozen men, some kneeling installing pipes, some standing clipping wiring, others dealing with the fire suppression system; it was a true hive of activity and enthusiasm. We called him the 'Circus Master'!

Tramontana was launched by Sara Quill, Jeffrey's daughter, in late June 1962 after which Jeffrey immediately took her to sea for the first time. It was a gentle run around the Solent to check the engine temperatures, look for oil leaks and generally see that all the systems worked properly. Our base for the trials was at the Vosper Yard on the Camber, a creek at the mouth of Portsmouth Harbour near the old town. In the days of the old sailing ships, Portsmouth, or Portsea Island, was a true island where sailors were allowed ashore because obviously, they could not run away or jump ship, particularly those men who had been shanghaid. Portsmouth has been known to generations of sailors from all parts of the world, for its pubs and girls.

On the main building slipway was a warship, a patrol boat for the Chilean Navy and, moored alongside the quay, was Peter's private yacht *Sea Victory*, which had started life as a Fairmile, a Naval motor launch and which he had converted after the war.

An intense series of sea trials then took place. As soon as we were satisfied that we could, with safety, open up the engines to full power it was evident that the super cavitating propellers were a bit too heavily pitched as we could not get 2,000 rpm. Two other sets of finer pitch propellers were ordered from the small propeller factory at Totton to replace them. The design of these super cavitating propellers was very critical as the forward surface of the blade is virtually running dry, the rear surface acting like a paddle. Vospers had their own propeller tunnel with a glass panel and a strobe light to enable the designer to see exactly what was happening to the water flow. Finally, the new propellers were well matched to the power and speed of the boat as we were getting 49 knots at 2,000 rpm when measured over a specific distance in Stokes Bay.

After a couple of weeks the press were invited down, the reporters being taken out for a trip round the Solent in *Tramontana* while the photographers were in *Swordfish*, a fast workboat. These pictures were disappointing as the weather was overcast and relatively calm and, being a clean running boat, it made little spray. *Tramontana* had been designed to be at her best in a rough sea and so it was proved later. Various friends of Dick Wilkins and Peter du Cane were taken out, including George Eyston, the holder of the World's Land Speed Record in the 1930's. I suppose it is hardly surprising, but those men who like fast cars, fast boats and aeroplanes, have the same tastes. Sheer speed sets the adrenaline coursing through one's veins.

During the course of these trials we found that at full speed in smooth water under the lee of the land, but with a strong side wind, there was a tendency to heel into wind, followed sometimes by a turn in the opposite direction. This swing could not be countered by use of the rudders unless it was corrected early before the divergence had time to develop; it was disconcerting and required an alert helmsman.

Under these calm conditions I found it best to keep the boat 'alive' by treating it like riding a bicycle by steering in a series of very gentle curves. In rough water she responded to the power assisted rudders in the normal way. Lack of directional stability had been experienced before on other fast patrol boats and it was thought to be due to the flow of water curving up the flare of the bow. Ultimately it was found to be so but not until after the race.

Peter was a generous host and he often entertained us to lunch on *Sea Victory*. She was a most comfortable boat with a large saloon on the upper deck where, over a drink, we could discuss the events of the morning trials and plans for the race itself. Peter had examined closely the wind and sea conditions to be expected in the Channel during

September and had concluded that the chance of a rough head sea was more than 50%, hence the relatively heavily built boat. If, on the other hand, it was misty or foggy he decided to include provision for a Decca Navigation system. Commander Michel was an expert in this field of navigation but the set required quite a lot of electrical power which involved a motor generator being mounted on the inside of the transom high above any bilge water but this was to cause trouble later.

After the work-up in the Solent area it was decided to make a survey of the course to Torquay and to take a look at the various landmarks en route. Dick Wilkins had a house at St Mawes in Cornwall and he suggested a working trip from Portsmouth. We identified various landmarks and the location of some fishermen's lobster pots which had a floating glass ball to mark them and which could easily damage our rather tender propellers. We decided to go very close to Portland Bill, literally 50 yards from the rocky point, as there is deep water there and the lobster pots only came to about 100 yards from the shore. The Skerries buoy in Lyme Bay near Dartmouth, our next mark, was quite difficult to find. If the race took place in rough water and poor visibility it would be especially difficult without a fix so we decided to install a Decca navigator.

Nigel Tunnicliffe, as skipper of *Sea Victory*, was accompanying *Tramontana* and had made arrangements with BP for us to take on fuel at Poole and Plymouth. We discovered, however, that a petrol-engined boat with 750 gallons of high octane fuel was not popular with the respective Harbour Masters although refuelling from a bowser on the quayside was not specifically forbidden in the rule book. When we reached Plymouth we were banished to some distant commercial jetty. Otherwise the journey to the west was uneventful although it gave us a chance to shake down together as a crew and to become familiar with the boat.

Picking up a mooring off Dick's house we were given a great welcome and in return we made one or two joyrides for some fishermen friends of Dick. Waiting for us at the top of the steps leading to the Mediterranean like patio was a sumptuous lunch and pint mugs, not of beer, but of champagne! This set the tone of our 24 hour stay as we were royally entertained. The next morning we set off to return to Portsmouth. It did not seem any distance cruising at 35 knots although down in the main cabin the motion made it impossible to read a chart or even have a drink without spilling it so we stood around in the sheltered part of the cockpit taking it in turns to drive.

Sea Victory, which had accompanied us, was an ex-wartime Fairmile M.L, 105 feet overall, with a narrow beam and round bottom but the wartime Packard-Merlin engines had been replaced with smaller diesels. Jeffrey Quill told me that she had had an interesting history as she was used by the Navy to collect boxes of ball-bearings from Sweden during the war when the engineering industry was very short. Sweden has the reputation of making the best bearings using their high quality steel. These dashes across the North Sea were made at night and at high speed to evade the German patrol boats as she was only lightly armed.

After the war she was used by Vospers as a suitable vessel for research and development into anti-rolling devices. The outcome was the building of roll damping fins, a gyro controlled system of lateral projecting variable incidence fins rather like the forward flippers on some fish which counters any tendency to roll. Modern warships are equipped with these to provide a steadier platform for helicopters and the guns, also on commercial craft such as ferries and cruise liners to reduce rolling on these rather top heavy, but big passenger capacity vessels, to improve living conditions.

CHAPTER XIII

Cowes to Torquay Race

Briefing for the race took place at the Royal London Yacht Club on the evening before the start. With the Daily Express sponsoring the race, Sir Max Aitken made the main speech of welcome to the competitors. At the end he warned the drivers to be extremely careful at the start as, although spectator boats would be asked to keep clear of the course, the ability to control racing boats, heavily laden with fuel and with small rudders, was not very easy in the unusually cut up waters. Long distance races are not won on the starting line but human nature being what it is, the aggressive competitive spirit is at full flood at this time.

He also told us that the forecast for the next morning was for a westerly wind of Force 5 to 6 which suited us as these were the very conditions that Peter had anticipated in designing the boat. Jeffrey and I also knew of the enthusiasm of the men who had built her and of Vosper's reputation, not to mention the backing that Dick had put into the venture. Dick was going to watch the start and then be flown to Torquay for the finish. It was up to us; we had to win! That evening Jeffrey and I went over our charts in our room at the Queens Hotel in Portsmouth in preparation for an early start in the morning.

We took the warning by Sir Max Aitken very seriously deciding to lie well back clear of the crowd. In fact it did not work out as, after waiting in Osborne Bay and creeping round Castle Point where the *Brave Borderer* was to commence the rolling start, we found that other competitors were giving us a wide berth and we had a clear run to the starting line at the Royal Yacht Squadron. Keeping the pacing boat, the *Brave Borderer*, just ahead on our starboard bow we held her in formation until she fired a yellow Very Light and sheered off to the north. We made a good start just in the lead.

The course was westwards from Cowes, past Egypt Point to the

East Lepe buoy, leaving it to port, returning past Cowes and Southsea and on round the Bembridge Ledge and south side of the Isle of Wight.

About two miles from the start and in relatively smooth water, *Tramontana* suddenly took a violent uncontrollable swerve to starboard. I knew that Sam Griffith, the American Powerboat Champion, driving *Blue Moppie*, had taken up a position close to our starboard quarter and I expected a crash at any moment but on glancing back I saw that he had just missed us by going under our stern. The rudders were completely stalled and Jeffrey was only able to regain control after shutting down the power and reducing speed to about 15 knots. However, all seemed well and we rejoined the leaders lying about third when passing Cowes. The cleared passage through the spectator boats was not wide and we made our way through cautiously and safely, although at least two rubber boats with enthusiastic photographers came more or less straight for us and we passed them at about the distance of a boat's length. We were relieved to draw clear in the more open water before reaching the Southsea mark. We again took the lead between Bembridge Ledge and Shanklin with *Blue Moppie* and the Italian boat *Ultima Dea* with Gianni Agnelli at the helm, in hot pursuit.

Although we did not know it at the time, *Tramontana* had been reported on the radio as having a damaged bow which gave Dick a nasty shock. In fact prior to the race the bow had been strengthened by fitting a metal plate on either side and what had looked like a damaged bow was in fact paint having been stripped off the metal by the sea.

Looking astern, after rounding St Catherine's Head, I saw *Ultima Dea* leaping off the big sea. During the preliminary tests, before the race, she had been tearing up and down in front of the Royal Yacht Squadron at Cowes making a tremendous noise. With three V-8 racing Maserati engines running at 5,000 rpm I personally did not give her much chance but Agnelli, the head of Fiat, was now driving like a demon, going so fast that on leaping off the water *Ultima Dea* was clearing the crest of the next wave altogether. How the boat survived I do not know but, ultimately, she finished third.

After rounding St Catherine's Head the westerly wind was building up quite a sea. Just astern of us *Blue Moppie* was making the most of the quieter water in our wake, in fact, Sam Griffith came very close to our stern nudging us to go faster and presumably hoping that we would possibly break something! Jeffrey was not to be pushed, however, and every now and then he would give the wheel a quick turn, the ensuing wiggle of which would throw Sam off line into the rough water either side of our wake. This would make him slow up leaving him a quarter of a mile astern but having come back into our slick he would soon come tearing up back into position. From ahead we could see his propellers clear of the water in these big leaps from wave to wave. Evidently he was in a hurry while we were taking no mean bashing in the prevailing seas either.

Along the mainland coast past Christchurch and Bournemouth, the sea was not so rough enabling us to increase speed to near maximum but *Blue Moppie* was not far behind. The Course took us to the landward side of the three Bournemouth Sewerage outfalls, not a pleasant sight, before turning south past Old Harry Rock where we had to elbow our way through a large number of spectator boats which had come out to see the race.

One of the hazards to racing power boats is the risk of catching a propeller in the lobster pot lines. We had been briefed as to the likely position of these but, although they trailed a floating line and a coloured glass float, they were difficult to see beyond 100 yards which was equivalent to only a few seconds warning. The first group of pots was in the vicinity of Christchurch but the odd pot can be found anywhere, even some way from land. The local fishermen were not keen to see us but with a sharp look out and an alert helmsman, lobster pots could be avoided.

Portland Bill could be seen some way off and we had decided to avoid the worst of the tide race which extends seawards up to three miles, by keeping very close to the point itself. With a bit of relatively calm water under the lee of Portland Bill, Jeffrey asked me to take over and we went in to within 50 yards of the rocks keeping an eagle eye open for the lobster pots. *Blue Moppie* was in sight astern and we received a pre-arranged signal from a friend on shore confirming that we were in the lead.

Round the headland there was a rough sea with a wind from the west of about Force 6. I had never handled the boat under these conditions before; it was a great thrill to brace myself in the driving seat, legs apart, one hand to the throttles, one for the steering wheel and get the best I could out of her. *Tramontana* weighed about 12 tons and I had the greatest confidence in the strength of her structure. Peter had borrowed a G meter from Farnborough and mounted it in the bow to measure the acceleration in waves. The weight and ballast water trim helped to get her through the crests but the pounding a race boat receives is tremendous and has to be experienced to be appreciated. After the race we found that the acceleration on the meter indicated that we had reached 25 G, that is to say that in the bow the weight of ballast water had increased 25 times and amidships, where the crew were located, it must have been about 12 times. People have broken their ankles when standing up and for this reason it is usual for the crew to stand with bent knees watching forward for every wave impact. *Tramontana*'s weight reduced the motion to some extent but it was not possible to read a chart in the cabin and difficult, even dangerous, to look backwards over the stern to take a back bearing, although Dick Michel did take one off Portland Bill when we were about three miles out into Lyme Bay.

Our course to the next mark, the Skerries, just south east of Dartmouth, was almost straight into the prevailing sea at a distance of about 46 nautical miles. After a few miles on a compass course the boat seemed to be making heavy weather of it, the natural pitch frequency of the boat conflicting with the pitch of the waves throwing us clear of the water. I found that by giving a sharp turn of the wheel as we climbed up the face of a wave, the boat heeled a bit and as it went over the crest with rudder applied, it lifted the stern slightly lowering the bow and, due to the slight change of direction, lengthening the pitch of the waves. All of this seemed to ease her motion, helping to reduce the pounding and increasing the speed. At the same time, as the propellers came near the surface on the wave crests and to prevent the engines racing, I pulled back the throttles, pushing them open again at the critical moment of the propellers getting a grip on the water again. It is vital to watch every wave and not allow the craft to become airborne to such an extent as to land back on the water with heel, so that half of the hull takes the full landing blow on the flat side of the vee bottom. This latter situation is apt to occur as the aerodynamic lift on the bow makes the rudder control less effective in maintaining direction and when airborne, of course, completely ineffective.

Driving, as described above, means that the course desired is not followed but, in effect, for part of the time, the boat is tacking into the waves. Although the sun was not out all the time I was aware of the stronger light from the west. I also knew that for the correct course the sun should lie 20° off our starboard bow. I was trying to make the highest speed through the water in a westerly direction and leaving the navigation until later when I knew we should see the Devon coast, probably near Bury Head. At this time the crew reported that the Naval

Tramontana. Oil painting by Cavendish Morton R.A.

Dick Wilkins, owner of *Tramontana*

Tramontana cockpit. Peter Du Cane, chief designer of Vosper Thornycroft with Jeffrey Quill, chief test pilot of Vickers Supermarine Spitfires

Cowes to Torquay Race. To the right above, HMS *Brave Borderer* pacing the start, 1962

Blue Moppie. Sam Griffith chases *Tramontana* off West Wight

Sam Griffith, American Champion in *Blue Moppie*, in a hurry off Bournemouth

Trident Number 103. Sonny Levi, designer. The start of 1964 Cowes to Torquay Race

Trident. Don and John Robertson, drivers, going eastwards to Southsea mark of course, 1964

Trident passing Hurst Castle. John Robertson, driver, 1965

The Nab Tower. Before engine failure, 1965

Patrol Boat, *Brave Borderer* was not far astern but there was no sign of *Blue Moppie.*

It was hard physical work handling the throttles, a vital control in a fast boat but I had settled down to the rhythm of the boat and the sea and was really enjoying the tussle. I felt at one with the boat and the sea with 2,000 hp under my hand and a fine fast craft parting the waves and hurling the bow wave as fine spray to the winds, with the rooster tail from the two propellers hiding the view astern. As we came in sight of the land into smoother water, we were able to increase speed again. Then we managed to get a fix from Bury Head.

I did not think that we could have been overtaken in the prevailing conditions from Portland Bill but I was anxious to get confirmation as, of course, we had been out of the sight of land for over an hour. A cluster of boats seemed to be lying where we expected to find the Skerries buoy and so it proved. We then headed north back along the coast to calmer water and Jeffrey took over. I was tired but elated, so were we all, but we still had no confirmation of our position in the race.

In that year's Race the course took us round Torbay past Torquay and along the coast to Teignmouth where we made a 180° turn to return to the finishing line at Torquay. Under the lee of the land in the calm water there were many boats out to greet us. One of them, with an enthusiastic crew, was a steamboat going flat out trying to keep up blowing his whistle and waving us on!

Because the last part of the race took us back over the same course we met our other competitors *Blue Moppie* and *Ultima Dea*, coming towards us so at last we knew exactly where we were placed before we finished. The Harbour Master directed us to the town steps on the quay where our wives and race officials were waiting. The other two boats came in and rafted up alongside and in a few minutes all the boats were swarming with people.

Peter, who had flown down with Dick after watching the start, was absolutely delighted. *Tramontana* was still fully operational, although the liferaft had broken its mounting and Lovegrove reported that the motor generator for the Decca Navigator had broken its mounting on the transom and fallen into the bilges, apparently still working away lying on its side. He had somehow secured it with a rope while still at sea and fortunately it had not damaged the bottom.

Dick was a most generous host and we had a great celebration that night in the Imperial Hotel. Ella had come down with a friend bringing a suitcase for me; she always thought of everything and that night I was particularly glad to have a bath and a change of clothes. The sweater which Ella had knitted me as a present before the race had shrunk by at least a couple of inches from sweat leaving a gap at the back!

Talking that evening to the Captain of *Brave Borderer*, which had also been designed by Peter, he said that he had had quite some difficulty in keeping up with us across Lyme Bay, even with his three 4,000 hp gas turbine engines but, of course, he had the responsibility of bringing his ship home safely while we were out to win the race. I remember Peter saying that their own testers never gave the boats quite the same rough treatment as the customers. He also said that the 35 knots which we averaged would not stand as a record for long. How right he was.

During the return journey to Portsmouth when we were half way across Lyme Bay we were intercepted by the *Brave Borderer* who warned us to keep clear of the firing range there. They did not know that we had a number of senior ex-Naval Officers aboard *Tramontana* who took exception to being given orders by the new, young, Naval personnel whom they knew personally and there followed a somewhat unusual but very personal, and typically Naval, exchange of signals!

During the war while flying from Boscombe Down, I had often used the Lyme Bay range, carrying out various aircraft armament trials including firing a salvo of 8 duplex rockets (16 rockets) while diving at maximum speed in a Typhoon. These aircraft came into their own when the Germans retreated after being encircled by the Allied Armies in Normandy. As each rocket head was a 4.5 inch Naval shell weighing 60 lbs, this load was the equivalent of a broadside from a cruiser, no mean weapon for a single seater aircraft. We were, therefore, well aware of the risks we might have faced had we strayed into the range area although these risks were negligible as I knew nothing was dropped without a good look round for boats. In addition it was peacetime and a Sunday with good visibility but the area was of course, marked on our charts as dangerous so they were quite right to warn us.

On returning to Portsmouth an investigation was made into *Tramontana*'s violent divergence at the start of the race. Other fast patrol craft, such as the Brave Class, did not diverge. They were bigger and much heavier than *Tramontana*, of course, with their three gas turbines of 4,000 hp each, two torpedos and 40 mm gun, although there had been reports of the rudders becoming very light at speed in calm water.

Peter du Cane thought that this behaviour was caused by the flow of water from the bow wave climbing up the inverted curve of the bow to the chine. The impression gained by the driver was of the boat suddenly being steered by the bow and the consequent yaw causing the outward heel, a potentially dangerous situation.

Peter had a new design of patrol boat on the drawing board with two gas turbines instead of three. This boat, ultimately to be called *Ferocity*, was on the stocks and nearly completed. He decided to alter the strakes or external appendages attached to the hull and to curve them upwards near the bow at right angles to the flow of water when planing at speed. Later *Tramontana* was similarly modified and subsequent trials proved highly successful in breaking up the boundary layer of water at this point with no further divergence problems being encountered.

The Cowes to Torquay Race was originally intended to improve power boat cruisers and all entries had, under the rules, to have a cabin, galley, head etc. The only other requirement, apart from safety measures, was that the boat must not exceed 40 feet in length but there was no limit on engine size. The international entries, largely American, which were attracted to the Race, had only the very minimum of accommodation and were really just decked in open boats. This was the type which had been established previously in the United States and had led to championship racing. It was after *Tramontana* won the Race in 1962 that objections were raised to the very big petrol engines and the rules changed which limited the size to 16 litres for petrol and 32 litres for diesel engines. The change in engine capacity was readily accepted for future races as a sensible compromise, both to encourage sponsors and to contain costs which in any case are very high.

Tramontana was in good order but no longer acceptable for racing in competition and she was not easy to sell as few people could afford to run her. Agnelli, however, impressed by her performance and partly because the engines were Italian, made a bid for her which Dick accepted. After a thin skin of glass reinforced plastic covering had been applied to the wooden hull as a protection against marine life, she was shipped out to the Mediterranean where she was used by Agnelli to beat up all the playboy speed kings with their Rivas. I heard that, under another owner, she finally struck a rock somewhere and sank!

CHAPTER XIV

A New Approach

For the 1963 Cowes -Torquay Race, Dick Wilkins decided to build another boat, *Tramontana II.* Under the new rules the first boat, *Tramontana I*, was no longer eligible with its two 57 litre CRM engines although its hull had proved to be most satisfactory. *Tramontana I* had been very strongly built structurally and, even though it had taken some very hard slams during the race, landing on the stern which was nearly flat, it had not suffered a great deal.

Dick wanted to use a British engine and so he contacted a number of knowledgeable people in that field whom he had known in his pre-war car racing days, and as a result Jaguar were approached. After their Le Mans wins, Jaguar's 6 cylinder engine was well proved on the road and powerful; they had increased the bore to increase the capacity from 3.4 litres to 3.8 litres and, finally, to 4.2 litres. This latter engine gave more torque to minimise the losses in the automatic transmission fitted in some cars but the smaller space between the bigger bore cylinders meant that the cylinder head gasket in that restricted area had to be very thin and it was for that reason that it was rarely used for car racing. Jaguars advised the 3.8 and after preparation by their racing department, were prepared to give a guarantee of 250 hp at 5,500 rpm for five hours at full throttle. Four of these engines would give 1,000 hp whereas the Americans would almost certainly be using V-8's with a maximum power of about 600 to 800 hp. However, as 1,000 hp was less than half the 2,300 hp of *Tramontana I*, for comparable performance, the all up weight would have to be halved.

Peter du Cane worked out his sums and came up with a similar looking boat but very much more lightly built and powered by four 3.8 litre Jaguar engines. *Tramontana II*'s new hull had a constant deadrise with a 20° vee bottom to split a wave on a heavy landing thereby cushioning the bump; this was similar to the American Ray Hunt design which was very successful. External strakes running forward to the upward curve of the bow overcame any tendency to swerve.

Each engine drove its own super cavitating propeller, the two outers mounted close to the transom with the power take off facing forward with marine ahead/reverse and vee drive gearboxes, the two inner engines facing aft driving direct, ie. without gear boxes, in order to save weight and which were normally closed down for manoeuvering. The brackets for holding the propeller bearings were mounted aft of the propellers and these also carried the four rudders. The engines were marinised by Vospers, each with its own heat exchanger and salt water pump. All the main pipes carrying fuel, water or exhaust were supported to relieve the connection of shock loads and in the case of rubber pipe connections each had two Jubilee clips to prevent them slipping off.

The fuel system consisted of two separate tanks each with its own shut off cock feeding to a common collector box just forward of the engine bulkhead. From these, four dual electric diaphragm pumps and filters fed each engine separately. The installation of four engines in such a confined space left very little room for access so all the instrumentation was placed under a perspex cover on the top of a locker at the aft side of the cockpit under the supervision of the engineer. The driver's seat as in the previous boat, was placed amidships with the navigator on his left hand.

The course of the Cowes to Torquay Race was changed for the 1963 event. Instead of going round the south side of the Isle of Wight, Southsea became the easterly turning mark and the boats made the return through the Solent past Cowes (for the second time), leaving via the Needles Channel. Scrutineering for compliance with the rules and equipment was on a barge moored off the Power Station in the Medina River on the Isle of Wight. A briefing, which included a forecast of rough weather, was given the evening before the race but all the competing boats had to pick up a card from the race control office on the morning of the race and display it in a prominent position on the windscreen. This was to ensure that every boat had been properly scrutinised and had not been altered since.

For this race, Jeffrey Quill and I had no navigator, the duty falling primarily on me. This was to save the weight of the Decca equipment and the operator. Lovegrove was engineer again with Sam Hutchins in charge of the boat. On the morning of the race we drove the boat, now named *Tramontana II*, over from Vosper's Yard on the Camber in

Old Portsmouth to Cowes and while I collected our authorisation card, Lovegrove changed all the plugs from soft, warm up plugs to the hard racing plugs.

The start went reasonably well but there was a great deal of bunching together at the Gurnard mark shortly after the start and we were lying about third after circling the East Lepe buoy before going eastwards to Southsea. We knew that our top speed was 39 knots and that some boats were faster but we banked on being faster in the rough water to come. After passing out of the Solent through Hurst Narrows, we turned right at the West Shingles buoy for the Christchurch mark. It was then that we saw from the rev counter that the outer port engine was not giving the full rpm. It was down about 1,000 rpm and running irregularly but it was very difficult to tell what the trouble was as the engine noise from the open exhaust from the four engines was deafening. We contemplated changing plugs but decided that the delay would be unacceptable and we did still have three good engines, probably giving about 36 knots. We seemed to be holding our position lying third and so carried on along the South Coast to Portland Bill.

After about 10 miles into Lyme Bay but while out of sight of land, smoke suddenly appeared from the engine cover vents together with the smell of burning rubber in the cockpit so we slowed to steerage way while Lovegrove made a quick inspection. He reported that the dynamo belt of No 3 engine had come off and this had run the adjacent belt which was driving the salt water pump for the heat exchanger, off its pulley. Without cooling on this engine we had to close it down but continued for a while on the other three.

Lovegrove thought he could replace the belts quickly so we cruised on slowly below hump speed and while doing so another boat came close past us and offered help but we waved her on. After ten agonising minutes Jeffrey told me to get Lovegrove out of the machinery space as he was going to open her up again. It was extremely dangerous down there with a lot of very hot pipes, whirling exposed belts and endless sharp edges especially as the boat was pitching and rolling violently in a rough sea. Lovegrove would not give up, however, and I tried physically to pull him out but he would not come. I saw that he was trying to fit another belt holding it with one hand on to the pulley flange and then pressing the starter! Jeffrey, exasperated, told me to tell Lovegrove that he was opening up and continuing regardless, and so he did!

With the other three engines we seemed to be making about

25 knots into the wind and rough sea but the motion was violent, the boat even leaving the water at times and appearing to fly with its relatively light weight and bulbous bow. After about 30 minutes Lovegrove appeared, bleeding and unable to speak but he had managed to get the engine going again and we were able to proceed at full throttle in the calmer water which we had reached under the lee of the land near Dartmouth. He told us afterwards that one of the long bolts holding the end plate of the dynamo together had worked loose jamming itself into the fan blades on the pulley and preventing the armature turning, a chance in a million considering that similar dynamos are fitted on most cars. How he had repaired it under those conditions was an amazing achievement done at great personal risk.

We finished third, which under the circumstances, was not too bad but on walking along the quay an official from the race committee told us that we had been disqualified for missing out one of the marks of the course! It was one of the worst moments in my life to find that I, as navigator, had made such an awful mistake. I felt dreadful to think that all those people who had backed us by their hard work and enthusiasm, had been let down; it was a terrible disappointment with only myself to blame.

I felt slightly better later when I discovered that a notification of change of course had been sent to the owner, Dick, some weeks before the race but I had never seen it. At the briefing meeting the chart of the course had been displayed showing the boats going round the Fairway buoy about one and half miles from the Needles but, because it had not been brought to my attention, I had not registered it.

On returning to Portsmouth, Vospers carried out some further trials on the boat especially as the port outboard engine was still down on rpm. They tried new plugs and an ignition check, they changed the rev counter and the sender, but to no avail. Finally they traced the trouble to the electric fuel pump which was a Lucas type with two diaphragms actuated by solenoids. One of the diaphragms was cracked and not delivering a full flow of fuel so that, at full power, insufficient petrol was being supplied to the engine, thus limiting its power by weakening the mixture at full throttle. The dual type pump was very difficult to check except on a test bench.

Tramontana II was ultimately sold to a friend, Peter Ricket, who continued to race her in partnership with Tim Powell. She was lightened off a bit to try to reduce weight further and they did attain more speed but the development of racing boats at that time was very rapid and she was soon being outclassed. They also had the misfortune while returning to Chichester Harbour, to strike a submerged wreck just to the east of the two Forts at the entrance to the Solent. I heard that she had sunk but was later salvaged to live another day.

CHAPTER XV

A Touch Of Breeding

By the winter of 1963/64 when my nephew, John Robertson, expressed an interest in power boat racing, I realised how much my own appetite for this sport had been well and truly wetted. In a sense it must be equivalent, for those who have a mechanical turn of mind, to a kind of technical Grand National. The development of these fast racing boats had very little application to commerce but it certainly helped to improve the conventional powerboat used for leisure purposes. Most of the participants were connected in some way with the boat building industry and I made many good friends. It is a very expensive sport and, understandably, at about this time it became much more professional and dependent on sponsorship by big manufacturers. The oil companies were also helpful in donating fuel for the big races which had been quite an item with *Tramontana I*, burning about 150 gallons an hour at full throttle.

While visiting Don Shead one day at Cowes, he showed me his three Volvo engined boat, *Trident*, designed by the well known Italian designer, Sonny Levi. It was laid up at Groves and Gutteridge's yard on the Medina at East Cowes but the three Volvo engines (hence the boat's name) had been removed by Shead and the transom converted to mount two only. Trident had already proved very successful in racing and had been substantially modified for the purpose. The driving position, at which one stood up, had been moved further aft, an extra 50 gallon fuel tank installed on chocks on the cockpit floor and a 50 lb lead weight built into the extreme front of the bow compartment to trim the craft; her weight was only 1.85 tons. I liked the look of her and as he only wanted £1,000 for the hull less engines I telephoned my nephew and asked him if he would be interested in sharing her with me which he was, and so the deal was agreed.

I had her towed over to Sparks Boatyard on Hayling Island and ordered two new Volvo engines. *Trident*'s history was well known to the manufacturers who promised to give us the latest slimline underwater units with splined output shafts to take the special bronze propellers, which we were advised to use by Don Shead.

Sparks Boatyard had a very good ex-RAF engineer who made a first class job of the machinery installation revising the fuel system and installing the latest ideas on exhaust pipe design which I can only describe as a 'bunch of bananas' type. The only snag was that the exit through the transom was rather low and with a full fuel load of 125 gallons one had to be careful never to leave the boat without a plug in the end of each pipe! Following Vospers' practice I had a perspex transparent panel let into the top of the engine covers to enable us to see the engines without opening the hatch while racing. As was shown later it proved to be a wise precaution.

Trident was ready for sea trials by the early spring. She proved to be an exceptionally good sea boat, very responsive and buoyant, so we concentrated on bringing the engines and propellers up to scratch. The engines were run in carefully, gradually being taken up to maximum revs. Our first set of propellers were not handed, ie. both rotated in the same direction, and we found that this caused a certain amount of bias on the wheel to steer a straight course, and, in addition, when the craft left the water on hitting a wave and the engines tended to race, the propellers on re-entering the water, gave a very violent kick to the wheel and, no doubt, threw a great strain on the control cables. On handing the output shaft on one engine to give opposite rotation, and with the new propellers, there was a significant improvement.

We had three months in which to get to know the boat and measure its performance. There is a convenient measured distance off Stokes Bay where, by timing our runs in both directions and making an estimated allowance for any tide, we were able to plot our speed at different engine rpm throughout the range. By making use of these figures it was possible to estimate, for instance, the time it would take to reach the Skerries buoy when crossing Lyme Bay from Portland Bill, a distance of about 45 nautical miles.

If visibility was poor, even in a head sea a rough estimate can be made of the distance run by estimating the average rpm of the engines. In addition I estimated the direction of the sun in relation to the course at half hourly intervals on the day of the race and painted lines on top of the foredeck at 10° intervals from fore and aft as seen from the driver's position. In that way, provided the sun was visible, it simplified navigation when out of sight of land, without relying on a swinging compass needle.

John, who worked in the City, had done his national service in the Royal Navy, serving in a Corvette under the navigating officer so, after my own mistake in *Tramontana II*, John assumed the navigation and we had no problem! While doing his national service, his ship had circumnavigated the whole of South America, returning to the Caribbean via the Panama Canal; some people have all the luck!

John very quickly became a good driver especially in rougher water where *Trident* was at her best and when I was beginning to feel my age! *Trident*, being a much lighter boat than the two Tramontanas, meant that it was essential to stand throughout the race ready to take the shock by bending one's knees. The driver's position had a wide strop attached to the lower part of the instrument board with a loop which went around the back of the driver's waist so that he had, by bending his legs, free movement in the vertical plane with something to lean back on.

Tramontana I had had a seat fitted which was adjustable for height and with arms which folded upwards and clear to prevent the driver being thrown sideways. In either case the steering wheel takes considerable loads when the driver is pitched forward on striking a wave. By the end of the second season in *Trident* the constant bending of the wheel, which was an aluminium spoked racing driver's type, broke off at the hub! I also found at the end of each season that one or two of my toe nails were black from the constant stubbing of one's foot into the toe of the shoe. The only solution was to cut the tip of the toe cap off.

Under the revised rules for competitors in the 1964 Cowes-Torquay Race, crews had to wear crash helmets and carry radio for emergency calls. The radios were transmitters as well as receivers which could float and therefore could be used in the event of the craft sinking and finding oneself in the water! All this was scrutinised the day before the race then afterwards we went alongside Souter's floating pontoon to be topped up with fuel as our consumption was to be measured, and a prize given for economy according to a formula devised for the Race. While topping up *Trident*, another boat which was just astern of us, overfilled his tank spilling petrol overboard. On pressing his starter to move off there was an immediate burst of flame and we had to make a very rapid exit from the scene. There were many fire extinguishers handy which brought the fire under control quickly and a tragedy was avoided but carelessness with all those boats heavily laden with petrol was unforgivable.

Having cleared the scrutineering and the briefing we were ready to start. The course had been altered again but the start was the same, passing the Royal Yacht Squadron line in a westerly direction. We made the final top up of the fuel tanks in the shelter of Osborne Bay before rounding Castle Point, but kept well clear of other boats, although there was a great deal of traffic especially on the return past Cowes in an easterly direction. The photographers were out in force, completely oblivious of the fairly obvious fact that a racing boat, while airborne, is not in control! On these occasions the helicopters also buzz around very closely producing some wonderful action pictures and, incidentally, are useful to have about in the event of any mishap!

The race went well for us and we won our class and also the fuel economy prize. We had one piece of luck as shortly after leaving the Southsea turning mark, I noticed a rise in the water temperature of the starboard engine. With the perspex panel let into the top of the machinery space cover, I could see the engine cooling water pipe had become disconnected and was merely squirting water at the hole in the cylinder block.

John throttled back the engine to a fast idle while I pushed the pipe, with its seal, back into position and by wrapping a piece of galvanised wire (an essential spare part in any boat) round the pipe, managed to hold it in place. The standard Volvo fitting was not bolted or held on positively and at 5,000 rpm the water pressure and the violence of the boat's movement was sufficient to dislodge it. I had previously put plastic bags over the distributors so the salt water spray had not shorted the ignition and we were very soon at full power again. We had also fitted an extra electric water pump to drain the bilge water from the machinery space. This operated continuously while at sea as any bilge water splashes up over the engine and is liable to cause trouble.

There is considerable skill in getting a power boat from A to B in the shortest possible time. The uninitiated may think it is a question of pushing the throttle open and hanging on and this may be the case in smooth water with a well developed, reliable marine engine, but continuous power for 4 or 5 hours is very different to a vehicle engine in which the driver lifts his foot for every corner thus easing the heat flow and sucking up lubricating oil into the cylinders. For this reason most marine petrol engines are de-rated to lower powers. For racing purposes the engine in calm water is operated at its limit. In rough water it is not possible to maintain full power without doing serious damage to the hull and, consequently, the engine has an easier life, except when the boat leaves the water and the sudden relief of the propeller load can lead to over-revving. Diesels have governors built into their injection pumps to prevent this happening but most petrol engines and especially ex-vehicle engines, do not and the driver must throttle back.

In some respects the two stroke engine, as usually employed in an outboard, has an advantage as it is not damaged by over-revving. With a four stroke inboard engine the valve gear cannot follow the cams at high rpm with the result that the top of the pistons may hit the head of the valves causing damage. However, the two stroke is less efficient and the fuel consumption per horse power is far higher, the lightness of the engine being offset by the fuel load in a long race.

The skill of the driver is in judging how far he can push the boat in a rough sea without breaking up the hull. As previously mentioned, figures of 25 G can be experienced and, when planing, the load on the bottom surface can rise to 2,500 lbs per square inch, no mean pressure! The choice of the best material is, of course, up to the designer but the bottom panels must be supported at close intervals if very thick plating is not used. The great advantage of aluminium is that it will bend and dent without cracking and it is for this reason that it is used in all types of road tankers in case of accident, particularly those carrying fuel or chemicals. In order to avoid 'hard spots' on the bottom, which is undesirable as it increases the hull drag, most racing boats rely for strength on thick outer skins leaving the baffles, but not the ribs, just short of the inner surface of the skin.

On examining the bottom of the hull of *Tramontana I* after the 1962 Race, it was very clear as to the exact location of the engines as the paint surface was cracking showing some flexing of the structure under the two engines. In *Tramontana II*, a much lighter boat, it was found that the whole cockpit deck had dropped by about two inches where it had broken away from the main amidships bulkhead which itself was undamaged.

They say racing improves the breed and one area in which this has occurred is in fuel tanks and systems. In the early years leaking tanks were a serious problem due to the fuel surging backwards and forwards in big tanks when the boat met a wave; closely spaced internal baffles solved this problem. The importance of supporting fuel and other pipes at frequent intervals minimises fractures from vibration. In the case of *Trident* which had an extra 50 gallon tank, this was a semi-transparent plastic circular tank mounted on chocks on the floor of the cockpit. It had no openings except the filler and suction pipe fitting on the top and had been cast centrifugally to eliminate trapping air bubbles in the glassfibre and so increasing its strength; it was also very light and incidentally did not need a gauge as the petrol could be seen.

The following year, 1965, we also had some success, again winning our class after a trouble free run through reasonably smooth water. On the return journey from Torquay it was blowing about Force 6 from the west but we decided to go anyway because John had to get back to work on the Monday morning and we did not want to leave the boat in Torquay. Nigel Tunnicliffe of Vospers, who had built *Tramontana I and II*, came and helped us and he was very impressed by the way *Trident* behaved. It was a day of bright sunshine and rough seas thrown up by the wind against the tide. We rounded Portland Bill a stones throw from the rocks, although in relatively calm water, but at the next headland, St Albans Head, to the south of Swanage Bay, there were some very big seas caused, probably, by a westerly wind against an adverse tide crossing a shallow rocky shelf which caused huge holes in the water. We passed a sailing boat, about 100 yards from us, on staysail alone but she kept disappearing as we tobogganed down one wave and up the back of the next. One felt quite safe in *Trident*; we were dry and in full control of the situation, enjoying the ride.

The particular conditions, however, made me realise why Peter du Cane was so very keen on buoyancy in the bow of a fast boat. The narrow raked bows of some racing boats look pretty and streamlined but they must be at risk of diving under water in a big following sea.

CHAPTER XVI

The Call For More Speed

During the winter of 1965/66 we realised that to remain competitive we needed more speed. The Volvo Penta engine was quoted as giving 125 hp but virtually the same engine was being used in sports car racing and there was considerable experience and knowledge of its further development. Having found where to go we removed the cylinder heads, complete with carburettors and I took them up to a workshop in the Midlands. I did not see the work that was done but I believe they ground out and polished the ports, fitted new valves (sodium cooled?) and shaved 1 mm off the heads to raise the compression a bit. I was told that it was not advisable to raise the compression ratio too much as cylinder gaskets would not stand it, the gap between the cylinders being rather narrow.

While the engine was being tuned I took the two bronze propellers to be coated with PTFE, the wonder plastic which had been recently produced by ICI and which had the coefficient of friction of ice and was anti-corrosive. Peter Leach, a good friend, who frequently sailed with me in our multihull, *Snow Goose*, happened to be on the Sales Staff and managed to get the job done for us but it was an experiment, it not having been tried before.

As we were making two alterations at the same time we had no way of measuring the effectiveness of each separate modification, something which one should never do. However, on running the boat again it was clear that we had much more power and speed. Previously the top speed in calm water was 33 knots. After these modifications we were getting 38 knots, a very satisfactory result.

The course for the 1966 Cowes-Torquay Race was again changed. After Southsea the boats were to head south east round the Bembridge Ledge buoy into Sandown Bay and then round a mark off Ventnor and again eastwards to circle the Nab Tower before passing through the Solent. The object of this diversion was two-fold, to bring it within the range of more spectators and also to make the distance similar to other major International Races.

Trident was in top form, she was well prepared and with more speed, our hopes were high. I took the first turn at the wheel and as the weather was relatively calm, started off very fast using 5500 rpm. All went well and as far as Southsea we were up with some of the slower Class 1 boats. Just before rounding Culver Cliff, on the east coast of the Isle of Wight, we saw in the distance a big cloud of black smoke; I knew what that meant from many past memories of flying. As we approached the fire we could see a boat was burning from end to end and the sea around it was also burning from the escaping petrol. There were two motor boats close to the wreck and we slowed up a bit in case help was needed but the crew had been rescued and there was nothing else we could do. After the race we discovered that the accident had been caused by one of the propeller shafts being broken, the broken end acting like a flail had cut through the main fuel pipe.

Around Dunnose Head the sea became rougher but I pressed on with the boat more or less flying and in perfect trim. The pitch of the waves must have suited her as we seemed to be skimming over the tops with no ploughing through it making a thrilling drive. I handed over to John shortly after and he certainly made the most of her extra speed, really letting things rip.

Shortly after passing the Nab and heading for the passage between the two Forts there was a sudden big bang from the port engine and we slowed up. The engine was idling but there was no drive to the propeller and on taking a look over the stern I could see that the vertical shaft of the outboard drive had come through the top cover. There was nothing to be done except creep back to our home base at Hayling Island on the other engine watching all the other boats passing us. It was annoying but largely my fault for going too fast at the start. We should have planned our race better as we really had a margin of performance in hand over our nearest competitor in our class but we had chosen instead to have a race with the big boys.

We had taken some big bumps before the transmission failed. The engine sump, although it had a 2 inch clearance gap, had been pushed in by hitting a steel mounting looped under the engine taking the weight at the forward end; a wise modification by Don Shead. The standard Volvo Penta mounting is bolted to the transom only, with no support under the engine itself; adequate for cruising but not for racing.

After the breakdown in 1966 we entered again in 1967 and finished second in our class being passed by *Yo-Yo*, another Volvo-engined boat. We had planned to return to Portsmouth on the Sunday after the race but the weather deteriorated and the wind increased to gale force. John and our respective wives returned to London by train as he had to be at work on the Monday morning while I arranged to bring *Trident* back to Hayling Island with the help of a young man, the son of a friend who lived near Torquay. In the event I had to stay three nights waiting for the weather to improve, finally deciding to leave on Tuesday. At that moment my prospective crew's mother stepped in and refused to let her son go which was a big disappointment to the boy who was only 16 years old.

I was keen to get back to London and so I decided to go alone, no-one else being available at short notice. There was still quite a sea running but the wind was behind me and I thoroughly enjoyed the three hour trip entering Chichester Harbour about an hour before dark to be greeted by an anxious Ella and my daughter, Jane. They had rung up the Coastguard for news and to my surprise I found that I had been tracked by them all the way up Channel. They even rang Ella at the boatyard to let her know that I had entered the Solent and gave her my time of arrival at Hayling within five minutes!

From time to time John used the boat for taking family and friends for a ride. I do not remember even using her cabin overnight although it would have been possible for two people because under the racing rules she had to be fully equipped including pots and pans etc. We had a head but there were no seats in the cockpit and the finish was pure utility, no floating gin palace, although the gin was there! It is thirsty work racing but I found that the movement and wind made it very difficult to drink from a glass or mug so we fitted a couple of bicycle drinking bottles of the type used by road racing cyclists. They have a plastic tube through the cap going down to the bottom of the container which fits conveniently into a spring loaded clip. Our usual choice was Coca Cola or bitter lemon with brandy and ginger ale as an alternative, in case we got wet of course.

One day five of us, John and his wife Jenny, Ella, Jane and I made a trip over to Cherbourg for lunch. The weather was a bit misty but there was little sea running and the trip from Hayling Island took about two and a half hours to Cherbourg where we moored up in the inner harbour near the Yacht Club. After a drink at a bar whose owner was a celebrated veteran of the Maquis, we went next door to the

Café de Paris for a smashing lunch; everyone was cheerful. On the way back to the boat we had time to pick up a few bottles from Henri Ryst and set forth for home at about 3 pm.

The trip home was uneventful except that the mist had come down a bit and visibility was only about one mile. Suddenly about mid-Channel a large black ship appeared dead ahead. After a quick sheer off course we passed 200 yards apart. The ship was the *Bremen* and was obviously going to Cherbourg having picked up passengers from the Solent but it was not one of the usual shipping lanes and came as quite a surprise. As we were both probably doing 25 to 30 knots our closing speed must have been about 50 knots or giving just 35 seconds to avoid collision. It sounds a short interval but whereas the *Bremen* could not change course quickly we were alert and very manoeuvrable so there was really no danger.

We entered for two more races to Torquay but the engines and the boat had had a fair thrashing by then and had become uncompetitive. Instead of being taken into the workshops for a complete overhaul, *Trident* was parked at Fairey Marine's yard in the open and given only the minimum of preparation. In spite of this we managed to finish in four out of five races and in one race finished seventh overall, including the Class I big boats. For this degree of reliability we owed Don Shead, now the designer of Sunseekers the well known fast cruiser, a vote of thanks and Sonny Levi, the designer of *Trident,* for the excellent handling qualities of the boat. Sonny Levi is still in the front rank of fast boat design as he was responsible for *Atlantic Challenger,* Branson's boat, which beat the time of the Blue Riband holder across the Atlantic, the liner *United States.*

Sponsorship of these Blue Riband Transatlantic fast boats seems to be leading to increased public interest and certainly as I write a great deal of money is being poured into them with both Vosper Thornycroft and an Italian firm, building challengers for the record. So far as practical application is concerned it is hard to see any commercial future but there is no doubt that the large number of leisure boats have benefited indirectly from the lessons learnt in racing.

The sport of powerboat racing has great visual attraction hence the interest by sponsors for advertising purposes. Most boats have quite large areas of flat surface suitable for painting the firms logo on and with the close up photography from low flying helicopters the maximum publicity and somewhat dramatic pictures can be exploited in the media and television.

By 1969 at the age of 61 and with a boat which had had a hard life I decided to sell *Trident* putting her up for auction at a yard in Poole. She needed money spending on her and I had other pressing interests at that time. Throughout the period of competing in the powerboat races I had also competed in races for multihull sailing boats including the first circuit of Britain in 1966. I had become an outside Director of Royal Doulton, the fine china manufacturer, which took up an increasing part of my time and involved a great deal of travel within the UK. In 1965 my friends had asked me to help set up a new hovercraft company, Hovertravel Limited which was to operate a public service for passengers across the Solent between Ryde and Southsea. As I was now participating in powerboat racing, multihull sailing and having to work for a living, an added commitment to Hovertravel meant it all became too much so I cut out all my active pursuits by selling *Snow Goose* and *Trident*. All these commitments, especially the work for Royal Doulton, had involved a great deal of driving but the deterioration of my sight made night driving particularly difficult as I had glaucoma.

When my daughter Jane married in 1965 Ella and I had decided to sell our house in Kingswood, Surrey and move to an apartment in London nearer the Doulton office and within easy reach of the main rail transport system. The setting up of Hovertravel, an entirely new system of transportation, involved a great deal of work both on the political and technical side not to mention the financial aspects. During these years Ella was occupied for several days a week with her voluntary work for the National Children's Adoption Association. She also played quite a bit of bridge but I was poor company usually arriving home feeling dead tired.

Jane had married an Army Officer who had been based in Malta but had had to return to the UK early as he had developed trouble with a knee which had been injured while playing rugby. This soon led to his being invalided out of his infantry regiment when he found a job with Rothman's Tobacco Company in South Wales where they bought a house. Three grandchildren arrived in rapid succession, Camilla, Guy and Matthew, born in 1968, 1969 and 1971 respectively and as South Wales was a convenient place to visit we managed to see quite a bit of them.

All these upheavals amounted to a change from an active life to a business life although my personal interest was still inclined to engineering and new inventions but I had to earn a living and sailing boats, powerboats and later pioneering the operation of hovercraft, did not make money! However Royal Doulton had five factories making different products (all ceramic) employing about 5,000 people and although my efforts were primarily concerned with financial affairs because of my knowledge of the City, I was made a Director of their research company where certain interesting developments were taking place.

We lived a quiet life in London but Ella, who had started to smoke during the war, began to have various health troubles as a result of her habit while I had a series of eye operations. It was a convenient place to live for both of us. In 1969, however, on returning from a weekend away, we were shattered to discover that a serious fire had occurred in the flat below, which burnt through our floor and eventually the entire inside of the building was gutted. We lost nearly everything. On returning to Paddington a Royal Doulton car with my nephew, John, met us. Ella and I thought something had happened to our daughter Jane but we were told that our home no longer existed. We were taken there and we just stood on the pavement with our weekend suitcase holding all our possessions, and feeling very shaken. Good friends rallied round and we were taken to Grosvenor House Hotel where a South African friend knew the manager. Our friend had come to stay with us, her arrival coinciding unfortunately with the night of the fire!

The next day she bullied the local Estate Agent into renting us a furnished flat. We were in deep shock and with no food, electricity or telephone, we just wanted to curl up in a dark corner and not see anybody. The next morning however, we went out for breakfast at the Kardomah Café in the Kings Road which was crowded with the youth of the sixties, all full of life and bursting with energy. The air was filled with the current rock and roll music and the whole atmosphere made us laugh at our crazy situation. This was the turning point for us and we gathered ourselves together.

Eight months later we bought another leasehold flat on the Cadogan Estate but the refurnishing and decision making for every item was hard work at our age, not like setting up a new home when one first gets married, and the cost took most of our savings. The comprehensive insurance was totally inadequate as usual. I had not read the small print and Ella had some beautiful antique furniture which had rocketed in price and in any event could not be replaced.

David Cooksey, my young sailing friend, came to our rescue and having helped with hanging curtains and pictures etc., helped us settle down again to a more stable life. He also fired up my enthusiasm for the 1970 Round Britain Sailing Race in which we competed in *Snow Goose*. It gave me a target to get fully fit again and in the following six months I did manage to throw off the low state into which I had fallen. It was just the right medicine and it worked but it was to be the last Round Britain Race for me and I sold *Snow Goose* soon after.

Part Three

HOVERCRAFT

CHAPTER XVII

Trial and Error

While sitting on the beach at Soller, a small harbour on the West Coast of Majorca, in 1959 I read a description of a new invention by Christopher Cockerell. His invention was an amphibious craft which lifted clear of the land or water by riding on a cushion of air. It was interesting because, although many attempts had been made to achieve this, none, to the best of my knowledge, had ever proved successful. My own experiences of speed on the water ranged from racing power boats to fast multihull sailing boats as well as seaplanes and flying boats, and I could appreciate the advantages of reducing drag by providing air for lift and using it as a lubricant. In addition there was the possibility of navigation over shallow water, debris and ice.

In my small workshop at home I had already made a number of small sailing boats so I decided to have a go at designing and making a small hovercraft myself. It had to be small owing to the limitation on the width of anything carried by road on a trailer but it also had to be light as the lifting power of the air cushion is, of course, dependent on the area and pressure. If the dimensions of the craft are doubled the area goes up as the square, ie. the lift of the cushion is quadrupled. The losses of air are, fortunately dependent on the periphery of the cushion which is only doubled. Put another way the bigger the craft the more efficient it becomes.

I studied what little published literature there was on the subject before setting to work on a one-man sized craft which was to be 6 feet in beam and 9 feet long. I could see the potential of the hovercraft and I was excited at the thought of being able to make one at home, making it work and being part of the pioneering of yet another form of transport.

I removed from my sailing boat the 40 hp Johnson outboard engine which only weighed 40 lbs or so once the outdrive and propeller had been removed. It gave an exceptional power to weight ratio but it had two disadvantages; one was that it normally used raw sea water, ie. cold water for cooling, and for simplicity the drive to the 30 inch diameter centrifugal fan had to be direct, but this limited the rpm to about 2,000 and consequently restricted the power available to half its total power or about 20 horsepower.

The choice of a centrifugal fan for lift was based on my experience with early jet aircraft fitted with gas turbine engines. All the British engines had centrifugal fans, largely because their design parameters were well established and their flow performance predictable, as opposed to the German engines which had axial flow fans the blades of which tended to stall. The drive shaft from my Johnson engine gave trouble as, of course, the fan had a great deal of inertia and starting up often broke the shaft. I had to use the standard shaft for the power take-off as the engine crankshaft had internal splines. In the end a centrifugal clutch in the hub of the fan solved the problem.

With the help of John Bennett, the Chief Instructor at the College of Automobile and Aeronautical Engineering at Redhill Aerodrome, we built the hull of plywood using wooden ribs similar to an aircraft wing structure. The ducts for the lift air which directed the air inwards at 45°, were also of aircraft type construction being of lightweight gauge aluminium. It was all very elementary but light and, rather to my surprise on finally starting up for the first time, the craft which we called *Skimmer I*, lifted about 4 inches. At a later stage it lifted five people off the ground, so my homemade fan design must have been quite efficient!

The method of control was for the driver to tilt the craft by leaning in the direction in which he wanted to go and operating a rudder bar connected with four internal rudders or guide vanes. The tarmac in front of the hangar at Redhill was ideal for testing as the surface was smooth and level and with no wind it was just possible to manoeuvre, although with no precision.

In 1961 hovercraft had great publicity value and the College, which was owned by the British School of Motoring, wanted to exploit their link with the project by inviting the BBC for a demonstration! I was most embarrassed as the craft was, of course, undeveloped and unreliable. In spite of my misgivings, however, the plans went ahead and quite a large party from the BBC and the daily press duly arrived. Somehow we managed to get through the demonstration without disaster and the next day there were a number of articles about homemade hovercraft explaining how anyone could make one in their backyard! The British School of Motoring had its publicity while I was left to answer many letters from interested schoolboys.

There were clearly many lessons to be learned as a result of building the first craft and the following winter I designed and made a second one. The control of hovercraft is difficult; it is the only vehicle which has no keel, fin or wheel to give it directional stability and therefore can move freely in any direction. This was, obviously, an area which required more thought and development so I decided to concentrate on controllability. The second craft called *Skimmer II*, had a two cylinder air-cooled two stroke engine out of another outboard.

The Excelsior Talisman of 28 hp had been designed for a motor cycle but as well as having, for a hovercraft, the advantages of air cooling, it had the additional advantage of an electric starter. For the sake of simplicity this engine drove an aluminium axial fan made by the Airscrew Company and both the engine and fan were located in the throat of a large venturi shaped duct mounted vertically on a similar shaped hull to the *Skimmer I*. The hull had a series of twenty vanes on each side mounted vertically and hinged at the top to allow them to swing fore and aft under the control of two levers similar to the control of the tracks of a bulldozer. I hoped these would direct the airflow escaping from the bottom of the craft in such a manner that the craft could be either turned on its axis or move forward or aft.

On attempting to start up the engine for the first time I ran into trouble as it would only fire on one cylinder in spite of every effort to find the cause. Like a fool, while the engine was still running, I leaned over the venturi shaped entry duct to feel which cylinder was hot and found my arm being sucked inward by the air flow. The axial fan's metal blades cut off the tops of my fingers on my right hand. Although they were cut off cleanly there was a nasty mess giving Ella a nasty shock. Roehampton Hospital did a very neat job in patching me up and I was able to return home in less than a week.

A month later on stripping the engine, the fault at last came to light. The crankshaft was a built up type and the two cranks, instead of being opposed to each other at 180°, were parallel so that on one cylinder the ignition spark was taking place when the piston was at the end of its stroke. The key on the tapered shaft had sheared allowing the two cranks to slip round into line with each other.

With the engine running properly the craft lifted off easily at about three-quarter throttle but, to my disappointment, the vane type control which I had hoped would make the air emerging from the cushion leave with a swirl, did not work and there was no response to the control levers.   I went back to the drawing board and designed special 'puff ports' which could direct the cushion air forward or aft and could be operated differentially for turning. This worked very well and gave good manoeuvrability even permitting the craft to be driven into the hangar and parked precisely.   However, the forward thrust was insufficient to propel the craft up even a gentle slope and was, for practical purposes, quite inadequate. We did demonstrate it at two or three aeroplane shows, including one at the RAF Battle of Britain Day at Gaydon and later that year at Shoreham when Dave Morgan, the Vickers Test Pilot, drove it, much to everyone's amusement.

The next year, after some thought and head scratching, I started on a third effort. This was based on a pneumatic or rubber dinghy type hull with two large centrifugal lift fans mounted on a transverse shaft with the exits pointing aft and a cut out underneath to the plenum chamber, or air cushion area under the craft. Control was by three rudders in each of the two fan ducts exits by a rudder bar and two swinging buckets over the top of the ducts which, by swinging over the duct exit, reversed the flow of air for forward and aft control. These were operated by two hand levers as with a tracked vehicle. The engine was a Villiers Starmaker of 25 hp, a single cylinder two stroke, normally used in cross county motorcycle racing.

Most of the trials I carried out were in my garden where various hazards, such as a grass slope, a fish pond and trees, provided quite a good test of manoeuvrability; these trials proved very successful. However on trying it out on the sheltered water of Bembridge Harbour in the Isle of Wight, it failed miserably as it lacked the necessary thrust to get it 'planing', not to mention the driver sitting in a shower of spray! I then added flexible rubber segments to the lower part of the hull but, again, these were not successful in improving the performance over water as the horizontal thrust was inadequate.

CHAPTER XVIII

Serious Business

In 1965 several of my friends and I became interested in starting a public hovercraft service across the Solent. The management and operation of Hovertravel Limited, as the new Company was called, took up a great deal of my time which meant that early efforts and experiments with small hovercraft were put aside to concentrate on the more serious commercial aspects of pioneering this new form of transport, which has now, after nearly 30 years, carried over 13 million fare paying passengers across the Solent.

Getting Hovertravel set up was quite an undertaking. Six of us raised £60,000 partly in the city, and we entered into a charter agreement with Westland Aircraft which had recently formed the British Hovercraft Corporation from their old subsidiary Saunders Roe at East Cowes. We had agreed to charter their new SRN6 Hovercraft which was just commencing production at the Westland Saunders Roe factory in East Cowes and which was designed to carry 36 passengers. My partners on this venture were the aircraft manufacturers Desmond Norman and John Britten, Edwin Gifford, a civil engineer and Mr Mann, a partner in Desmond's aerial crop spraying company, David Webb well known Chartered Accountant and myself. We were all keen sailors and innocently thought it would be fun to start using this new invention of Christopher Cockerell's.

The Government, meanwhile, had decided to consolidate all the big manufacturers who were interested in Hovercraft so that they could deal with just one company. British Hovercraft Corporation became the chosen instrument of the Government and all development work was given to them.

Before we started Hovertravel, another company, Hover Transport, had had a similar idea to run a service across the Solent by which the hovercraft were loaned to them by BHC to operate from Eastney near

Portsmouth to the beach at Appley, Ryde. Hover Transport was a private company but it only operated for three months in the summer of 1964 using Westland's SRN3 and SRN5. Hover Transport took their expenses out of the takings, the remainder going to BHC, but it was not really a viable proposition and a number of the employees, drivers, engineers etc. came and joined us at Hovertravel.

To operate a public transport service across the open sea is a serious undertaking as I soon found out for myself. We had different County Councils at each end of our route from Ryde to the mainland and a great deal of resistance to a noisy hovercraft. Mr Gifford had recently completed a feasibility study of a road bridge to the Isle of Wight so he already knew the existing traffic figures. He was also acquainted with a number of Councillors who were sympathetic to the idea but there were many shop keepers who raised objections. Presumably they thought they might lose business if Island people began going to the mainland to do their shopping.

The legislative position as regards the manufacturer and operation were necessarily vague as the Government itself was divided. The politicians thought it might give employment to possibly a large number of people but with Westland, Vickers and Denny Shipbuilders showing interest it led to disagreement between the Air Ministry and the Board of Trade. The public in general thought it was a great joke, 'was it an aircraft or was it a ship?' For Hovertravel, however, it was no joke as we had to deal with so many authorities apart from the two Ministries mentioned above. It involved the permission of the Isle of Wight, Portsmouth and Gosport Councils together with Trinity House which is responsible for the safe navigation of sea vessels round our coast, Radar Control as well as a number of others responsible for public transport.

On the whole these officials were reasonable about our request for permission to operate but the major concern to us and to others was the noise factor. The SRN6 was really designed for military purposes with little regard for quietness. Also it was, with its gas turbine and aircraft propeller, exceptionally noisy when manoeuvring at the terminal. I found myself pleading our case at Gosport and Portsmouth Council Meetings and at the Ryde Ratepayers Association in one day. I called upon their sense of patriotism to allow this new British invention to have a trial and in order to achieve this we had to have a route. In the end they gave us permission to operate for one year between Ryde Bus Terminal and Southsea beach near the amusement park.

Originally we had made preliminary plans to run the new SRN4, a car and passenger ferry, between Stokes Bay, Gosport and the western end of Ryde beach, as we had heard that the Council were considering an extension of the main road from the Golf Course down to the sea, joining up with the road on the front. This plan of ours was abandoned when the Government decided to buy this SRN4 hovercraft for the nationalised British Rail who at the time had a monopoly of ferry services around the British coast. Their idea was to operate it across the channel in competition to the Swedish company which had bought the first SRN4.

As a result we were forced to cancel our financial agreements in the City and settle for a route from Ryde to Southsea using the SRN6. In hindsight I am very glad we were prevented from acting on our original ideas.

We had to train our own staff to drive the craft but there was no legal requirement or licensing regulations as we were setting a precedent, there not having been a commercial hovercraft operation previously. The Government, in its wisdom, decided to treat hovercraft as aircraft for the purposes of the driver and although there was no specific test or licence we were instructed to obtain the agreement of the manufacturers, Westland, to accept our drivers as capable and responsible operators. Peter Ayles, a pilot from Britten Norman, had some experience with the cushion craft company owned by Britten Norman who made small hovercraft and he ultimately became our senior driver and Operations Manager.

The engineers were all ex-RAF as were the other drivers. Tony Smith, an ex-V Bomber Pilot and Peter Atkinson, an ex-Fighter Pilot joined the company on 2 August and were the first two to be trained by Peter Ayles who had to drive ten hours a day when the service first began. He was teaching the new drivers in the early morning before the regular service commenced. The staff operating the terminals were recruited locally and comprised two shifts, both for cashiers and beach staff.

Under the agreement with the Councils no buildings were to be erected so we had to use a large caravan at each end as a ticket office. As the staff grew in size we advertised for a manager which proved to be unwise as we were inundated with applicants all of whom were without experience although they had great enthusiasm for hovercraft. In the end Mr Peter Pralle undertook to manage the operation with the assistance of the Office Manager.

Mr Gifford designed the terminals, the existing slipway at Ryde being extended laterally like a fan which proved to be very successful as the tide sweeping up and down the Solent kept it clear of any debris while the Southsea Terminal had to be bulldozed clear of shingle after every storm.

As it was situated outside Portsmouth Harbour there was no complication with Naval or Harbour authorities and being next to Clarence Pier it had easy access for cars and parking as well as being in sight of spectators walking along the promenade many of whom became our passengers.

Besides the Southsea to Ryde route we had decided to operate a passenger service between Stokes Bay and Ryde at the same time but as we only had the one craft we had to alternate the route. After about six months it became obvious that the public preferred to travel from Portsmouth rather than Gosport, and so the Stokes Bay/Ryde route was gradually phased out. The inauguration of Hovertravel was on 4 August 1965 when Lord Mountbatten, the Governor of the Isle of Wight, consented to open the route and the Mayors of Portsmouth, Ryde and Gosport attended together with the Managing Director of BP who was helping us financially. It was an anxious day for us in Hovertravel as we had no reserve craft in the event of a fault developing. However, we had erected a large marquee on the beach, the sun came out and we had a good lunch. After Lord Mountbatten had made his speech and Peter Ayles, our senior driver and at that time, only driver, had arrived in the Hovercraft, the party of VIPs were taken on a trip across the Solent. All went well but even so when the big helicopter arrived to take about 20 people back to London, I heaved a sigh of relief.

Delivery of the SRN6 to Hovertravel had been made a few days before and we wasted no time as it actually went on the route the very next day. We found a steady stream of passengers keen to try this new form of transport. The craft had never had such intensive use before, each round trip taking about half an hour and we were running the service about six times a day.

This intensive use soon showed up weaknesses in the craft, however. The flexible skirt of an early type, known as the jet type, was in continuous trouble and we had to take the craft back nearly every night to the Westland's slipway at East Cowes for repair after completing the day's service. About six of our engineers had spent half of each night clambering in and out from under the wet skirt patching and repairing them, a thankless task.

It was only the determination of all the men concerned that made it possible to bring the craft up to a serviceable condition for the next day's operation. This enthusiasm to prove that this new form of transport would work was in fact felt at all levels throughout the company; without it Hovertravel would not have survived.

Within the next two or three months, Westland supplied a different design of skirt. This had a series of separate segments round the periphery and was a great improvement although we often had to hire a big mobile crane to lift the craft on the pad at Ryde for repairs. Somehow we managed to keep the craft running until the autumn when the second craft arrived. By this time we had carried 100,000 passengers, in six months but the revenue was just about breaking even with the costs.

With the coming winter and longer hours of darkness, we had to install radar. This was difficult as the hovercraft can point in one direction while moving in another and really needed a north seeking radar for which we required more electrical power. As an alternative we leased a portion of the roof of the Esplanade Hotel on the seafront at Ryde and with the kind permission of the owner, Mr Hayward, we installed our radar there.

We must have been the first private company to own its radar which gave very accurate information of all the shipping on that part of the Solent. The operator was in fact one of our drivers who was in constant touch with the driver of the craft and behaved as if he was sitting next to the craft's driver, reporting to him if there was any obstruction ahead or converging traffic.

The early drivers were all ex-Royal Air Force pilots and it was therefore natural to call them pilots but a certain amount of confusion arose because other people referred to them as drivers. This was just another of the confusions which arose out of the question of whether it was a ship or an aircraft.

When I made a small one-man hovercraft I was referred to the Air Ministry for a 'permit to fly' or in other words a licence to drive it. On going to the office of the issuing department of the Air Ministry, at that time located in the Strand, I was duly issued with a licence to drive a hovercraft subject to various conditions. The licence was in fact, an aircraft flying licence but with all the inappropriate limitations like flying heights over towns, etc. deleted. Later, when a meeting was called at the Air Registration Board, I represented Hovertravel and I queried the legislative position as to under which laws the meeting had been called as I had been under the impression that there were not any! Although perfectly friendly the Chairman of the meeting did not answer my question. From that time I suspected that the government had no legal authority over the control of hovercraft but was acting with bluff and intimidation. However we had many other problems to do with the operation so we always adopted what seemed sensible and commonsense to us. For instance we dealt with the question of passenger liability by taking advice from BOAC's legal adviser taking out 36 individual personal accident policies for £30,000 in blank names (one of our shareholders was C T Bowring, the well known Lloyds marine underwriter).

In 1967 British Rail set up a Hovercraft company called Seaspeed to train personnel ready for the operation of the big SRN4 which they now owned. For training purposes they used the same make of craft as ours, namely the SRN6, and began operating it between Cowes and Southampton where in fact, the hovercraft was not necessary as they had no sand bars or restrictions on the route and there were good harbours where an amphibious craft was not required. Financially it must have been run at a great loss so they decided to come to Ryde and made plans to have a terminal built near our own. We objected strongly, of course, taking the case to the House of Lords to get it squashed, all at our own expense! This happened after we had been operating for several years during which time our own route Southsea/Ryde was not proving to be profitable during the winter months.

CHAPTER XIX

Technical Struggle

The passenger traffic and revenue fell to one twentieth in the winter compared to the summer figure. Our Managing Director at that time was Christopher Bland who, after negotiations with British Petroleum, obtained a contract from Seismographic Services Limited to search for oil which was near to its peak price. We decided to form a new company, Hoverwork Ltd, to undertake all the operations of Hovercraft, other than the Ryde to Southsea passenger route, and soon it was proving a steady source of revenue.

Searching for oil is relatively straight forward on land and from a ship at sea, but in shallow waters around the coast, it is difficult and expensive. The hovercraft had about ten hours endurance and could carry all the electronic equipment and the explosive charges in racks on the sidebodies deck. In some areas we towed a floating cable about a mile long which, with the electronic sensors, even gave the depth of any oil field as well as the area. For the next 15 years we were engaged on this work around the coasts of every continent. (see appendix A)

We had a good working relationship with the British Hovercraft Corporation and Westland and as the demand for seismographic work varied we were able to charter additional craft. Meanwhile, on the Solent Ryde to Southsea route, the manufacturers were developing their skirt systems and trying them out on our craft. With each craft doing 10 hours a day, 364 days a year on the identical route, it was the ideal way of comparing various types of skirt without Westland or BHC having to run their own test craft. To my knowledge five different configurations were developed in this way.

Apart from the skirt designs the SRN6 had many alterations but BHC's technical director, Mr Boddington, who had worked for many years at Farnborough and also at Blackburn Aircraft, liked to make as few modifications to the original design as possible. This led to various disagreements when faults came to light as a result of our intensive use of the craft.

There were two particular features in the design of the SRN6; the first one was that the engine lubrication system was used to actuate the jacks of the puff ports located some distance from the oil tank which was in the engine compartment. If the oil tank was topped up to the brim, the oil in these long pipelines would overfill the tank on starting up. The vent pipe would then spray the surplus oil into the engine intake with the result that the engine would light up the additional fuel and overheat the turbine blades. The result was a very expensive engine burn-out.

The other weakness was that the hull fittings, which held the struts of the sidebodies, were machine forgings of aluminium alloy. We had a number of them crack from fatigue with some failing completely. One day in the autumn of 1966 we had three fail which left the sidebody being held in place by only three out of the six. I was so appalled, especially as we had 25 passengers on board, that I called upon the Air Registration Board, whose local representative was a Government Inspector, to ground the craft as they would have in the case of an aircraft fault of similar sensitiveness. He would not do so, however, so I decided to send both our SRN6s back to BHC telling them that we would not have them back until they had been properly modified. It was a very painful decision to have to make because it meant closing the service, laying off about 20 engineers and putting the drivers on half pay. I discovered afterwards that the Government Inspector could not have grounded the craft as he had no authority to do so due to the fact that there was still no legislation covering hovercraft.

As a result of this action we had no craft or revenue for about two months but when they were finally returned to us they had forged steel fittings on the hull and a new type of skirt which, ultimately, was called the segmented type and which gave a far superior performance to the original.

In my opinion the original design had not been sufficiently tested before being given a Certificate of Safety for carrying fare paying passengers. However we were able to re-employ many of the loyal engineers and staff and from that time onwards we were really in business.

Maintenance was expensive, each craft having to have a complete major overhaul every year while the Rolls Royce Gnome gas turbine required them at even shorter intervals. Westland used the same engine in their Naval helicopters where reliability is vital. Ours were not subject to the same flying certification and we were ultimately able to run our engines for twice the length between overhauls as those used by the armed services because hovercraft, in the event of an engine failure, could simply come to rest on the water.

Rolls Royce were very expensive so after two or three years we decided to overhaul our own. Any crashed or redundant engines that became available we bought, largely for their turbine blades. The Gnome is a beautiful piece of engineering, rather like a good Swiss watch, but running it in a salty spray does it no good at all. We used to wash the air intake filters daily and used various other techniques to clean the turbine blades. Our own engine overhaul business developed rapidly as it was much cheaper than the Rolls Royce manufacturer's price. We also hired out engines to customers while we overhauled their own.

When we undertook overseas contracts we always sent our own drivers and engineers to control the operation. It could be a bit hard on those with families but for the younger men it was a chance to see the world with all expenses paid, although sometimes the living conditions were dreadful. Their accommodation could be a caravan in the desert, 50 miles or more from civilisation, or a tent in a jungle or even on an icebound island.

They usually went abroad for three months only, before being relieved but if the charter was for a longer period, for instance in Australia, they were able to take their wives too, at the company's expense. Nevertheless it was a difficult job with some risk almost always in the inhospitable areas.

The surveying equipment consisted of about 14 electronic black boxes pouring out paper with all the data. This would be sent to London for assessment and analysis but of course the information was secret so we never knew whether oil had been found or not. Much later, when the price of oil declined, we obtained charters from British Gas which meant we were employed in the North Sea off Cromer in Norfolk and later in the sea off Blackpool.

While these overseas operations were going on, the Ryde-Southsea service was very gradually increasing its number of passengers attracting mainly professional business people and students which is still the case today.

A new type of hovercraft had been developed by the Hover Marine Company in Southampton called the HMII and when the old established Red Funnel Company, which operated a service for cars and passengers between Cowes and Southampton, wanted a faster craft we contracted to operate this new craft for them. We ordered the new HM, a sidewall craft which was propelled by water propellers and was not an amphibian, in 1968.

We put down a deposit of £15,000 on the craft but its completion was unfortunately delayed and the price went up. Then the government came into the picture with Seaspeed and as they were in a position of being able to pay full price, they took the HMII over and ran it from Cowes to Portsmouth. It was over a year before we received our deposit back.

The Hovertravel Board wanted a larger craft so Vosper Thornycroft were contracted to build a 300 passenger/car hovercraft, VTI, at a reasonable price, £1,000 per seat. They found the building cost was exceeding this price while the money we originally had available had diminished. In addition, when it was launched it was down on the specified speed so as we could not pay for it and they had managed to find an alternative interest from the Navy, we cancelled the contract by mutual consent.

These two set-backs, the VTI and the HMII, gave us the opportunity of reconsidering the craft situation. The VTI and the HMII craft were not fully amphibious while our own SRN6 from BHC was, so we decided, at that point, to concentrate on a fully amphibious craft only, leaving the cheaper sidewall craft to others.

On 4 March 1972 Hovertravel had a tragic accident when, on a scheduled trip from Ryde with 25 passengers on board, the hovercraft capsized on approaching the terminal at Southsea. There was a strong south-easterly wind against a fast running, six knot tide coming out of Portsmouth Harbour, making the waves exceptionally steep and short. Mr Course, the driver, had been swept off his line of approach to the landing pad and in manoeuvring to get into position for a second approach, the port sidebody dipped into the water while the wind on the opposite side, lifted the craft up and over on its back. With the watertight compartment in the hull bottom, the buoyant hull floated, but upside down a few inches above the water. The accident had been seen by the crew of the Marine Pilots Boat moored near Ryde pierhead and they were the first to arrive at the scene. An off-duty coastguard with his portable radio, who happened to be walking on Southsea Promenade, alerted the whole Solent area which meant that a helicopter from Thorney Island, workboats from Portsmouth Harbour and the Navy arrived within minutes.

By this time most of the passengers were sitting on the upturned bottom of the craft. The captain and a number of yachting people who had been aboard the craft had knocked out the windows allowing the passengers to escape, the forward door being below the water. This meant that the passengers were now in the water and those who had more experience of the sea helped them clamber onto the hull.

The wreck was ultimately blown ashore within a hundred yards of the terminal and naval divers were able to enter the cabin. Five people were missing according to the ticket check point at Ryde and tragically this proved to be correct, two of whom had been swept away by the tide.

My wife, Ella, and I were in London at the time the accident occurred but we caught the next train to Portsmouth and went directly to the scene where we found Chris Bland, Desmond Norman and the MP for the Isle of Wight, Mr Mark Woodnutt, supervising the rescue and visiting the hospital. The Navy sent a tug to tow the wreck out of the channel which was a difficult operation as it tended to be dragged under unless the speed was reduced to a slow crawl.

The next morning the media were there in force and I did my best to answer any questions. We had been operating regularly for seven years and up to that time we had had no indication that, with its great beam, the SRN6 could be turned over. Because of the confusion over whether it was a ship or an aircraft the original life-jackets supplied with the craft were of the aircraft, blow-up type, stowed under each passenger's seat. They were discarded years later in favour of the standard Board of Trade type which were much more bulky and rigid but more practical for older passengers.

BHC, previously Westland, immediately started a technical investigation. It was at this point that the legislative authorities realised that, although under the Hovercraft Act of 1972 it ruled that a Hovercraft was not a ship nor an aeroplane, they had failed to take any further action so they had no legal power to order an investigation into negligence nor did they hold any other authority over hovercraft.

The only public investigation was by the Portsmouth Coroner who ultimately dealt with the case and was satisfied that it was an accident and that no-one was to blame. He even said that the craft's built-in safety and equipment measures had functioned well congratulating Captain Course on his behaviour on saving the lives of so many of his passengers.

There was of course a very thorough technical investigation which made certain recommendations while we ourselves decided to continue the service instigating our own limitations. We had completed 13,000 crossings of the Solent safely but for the future we limited the service to certain weather conditions and set a cancellation figure of a 30 knot wind. We also decided to modify the sidebodies by adding a large luggage container into the outer part of each sidebody. These were used only occasionally as luggage carriers but we considered that the increased lateral stability provided by their buoyancy, was a wise precaution.

For the following few months I was kept busy dealing with endless problems in connection with the accident and I had many a sleepless night. Although the number of passengers travelling was down in the week immediately following the accident, it soon picked up. The very day after the accident I was surprised and delighted to hear that the Mayor of Newport, Mr Bailey, and his wife had bought return tickets, travelling to Southsea and back as a demonstration of their confidence in the service. It was a gesture which I and all personnel in Hovertravel are never likely to forget.

In double quick time the Government introduced a very extensive programme of legislation for Hovercraft. This served to cover everything from the safety aspects and the technical side of its operation. However when we later took one of our craft to Holland under its own power, the Captain received a radio message while at sea to return to the UK. The Government had realised that they had international commitments to adhere to concerning safety at sea, licensing of crews etc., and they had still not thought of the Hovercraft as an open sea-going vessel which would travel outside British territorial waters. The captain put into Pegwell Bay on the Kent coast and rang up to find out why he had been recalled. He was told that, as he had no sea-going licence, delivery of the craft to Holland was breaking regulations but in fact he was an ex-Captain of the Red Funnel Ferry service to the Isle of Wight and had a Master Mariners Certificate! This illustrates the confusion that still existed as to the status of the hovercraft even though we had been operating for nearly a decade.

The new legislation placed Hovercraft under the Civil Aviation Authority (CAA) for technical matters and the Board of Trade for Marine matters which meant we had double the number of authorities with whom we had to deal. This confusion often led to regulations being duplicated such as when the CAA called for the suppression of fire in the machinery space by flooding the area with inert gas as in aircraft, whereas the BOT called for a metal box to contain the fire for

15 minutes to give passengers time to embark into the ship's lifeboats. Hovercraft, it was decided, had to have both methods and this is still the case today! Having experienced two fires myself, one during the blitz and one in my apartment in London, I am in favour of having both regulations in force.

Members of the public, as well as others who should be able to appreciate the difference, think only in terms of speed on the water, but the fully amphibious type opens up a completely new market. The third world is full of un-navigable rivers and requires transport but they have little money so we decided to concentrate on special applications, such as work boats, ice bound patrol and rescue boats as well as coastal patrol boats (drug and smuggling). The hovercraft offered special advantages; as an example, while the contractors were building an island in the Wash to measure erosion by the sea with a view to building a reservoir out there, we ferried men and some equipment at all states of the tide and completion was speeded up saving costs. One day we had a surprise visit by Princess Margaret and her children for a trip round the Wash!

In spite of complaints about the noise of the SRN6, the various councils allowed us to continue operating, but pressure on us to take action with respect to the noise was increasing. The Vosper Thornycroft original design, VTI, which we had wanted to buy, had submerged water propellers which would have made our operation quiet but, after these plans had fallen through, there was little we could do immediately to reduce the noise of the SRN6 because Westland had refused to modify the air propellers. The naval version of the Vosper VTI was fully amphibious and had air propellers but they were ducted which made its operation quieter than ours. As a result of this disappointment we decided to modify our SRN6 to enclose the propeller in a duct which would reduce the noise factor by roughly 50% but it did not meet with the approval of Westland and the proposition was dropped.

After these set-backs the Board of Hovertravel decided to make a feasibility study of a totally new design which would meet our own requirements, a 60 passenger craft with two diesel engines and fixed pitch ducted propellers. The hull was to be of welded aluminium which would make it heavier but would also avoid the cost of millions of rivets which are necessary for the very thin sheet of the SRN6.

BHC, however, was not interested in building another hovercraft for the civil market, stating that in their opinion, diesel engines were far too heavy and impractical for hovercraft.

We sought the help of Mr Winter, the designer of several smaller hovercraft, and decided to go ahead ourselves, subcontracting all the major parts, such as the hull, to Fairey Marine. The National Research Development Corporation, originally financed by the government to assist with new inventions, agreed to find half the money for this new design and to match our own input of about £250,000.

The final design was for 80 passengers, twin engines for thrust, and two more of lesser horsepower, for lift. The engines were of the Deutz German design ie. air cooled diesels. Air cooling avoided using radiators which would otherwise have been necessary as a hovercraft is entirely above the surface of the water and cannot, therefore, take in fresh salt water from the sea for cooling. The figure of 80 passengers was later increased to 100 passengers but for any figure above this, the legislation required a larger cabin crew for safety reasons.

When the hull had been completed the NRDC called a meeting which David Webb and I attended. We were told that the NRDC money was not available unless the whole project was handed over to BHC! There was no real explanation for this drastic change of mind but I knew there had been a bitter fight over the segmented skirt licence between Hovercraft Development Ltd, financed by NRDC, and BHC, so it was possible the two were linked. This decision left us no alternative but to go to BHC who agreed to take over the final financing. This craft was then called AP188, or Advanced Product 188.

Although the basic design was Hovertravel's no credit was given and it became a BHC craft. My co-director, David Webb, in another capacity, was Chairman of Calcutta Trams and Beechams and was highly regarded in the city as a company 'doctor', often called upon to put failing companies back on the road to profit. The matter was smoothed over in the end mainly due to the fact that David had become good friends with Walter Oppenheimer, the Finance Director of Westland. They had developed a mutual respect for each other during the negotiations in the very early days over Hovertravel's debts for spares and Westland's costs.

Technically the AP188 was a great success and transformed the finances of Hovertravel with its increased capacity (100 passengers) and lower operating costs. This was caused by lower fuel consumption of the diesel engine and the welding of the hull instead of rivetting which reduced the maintenance costs by half while seat mile costs were down to about a quarter of the SRN6.

CHAPTER XX

Diverse Operations

In 1967 we had been asked to provide a hovercraft service for passengers between the City of Montreal and Isle Charron, the site of the Man and His World Exhibition. We were confident about providing this and considered it to be a good opportunity to show a new British form of transport in North America where they had no equivalent craft. We took both SRN6s from the Solent run, chartering others temporarily from Westland in order to keep the local service going.

The Montreal project entailed forming a Canadian Company with a majority of Canadian Directors, getting permission from the Montreal Harbour Authorities and even constructing special terminals. A retired senior Canadian Naval Officer joined the Board and with his help the various Government authorities who had to give approval for us to operate, co-operated. We also needed a maintenance base which was about two miles away but in Quebec Province.

All this activity diverted much of our effort from the UK operation but I felt it was important to look for new markets overseas, especially in Canada where I had spent three years flying mail to the North. The short route to the exhibition was operating well until, about six weeks after we had begun, one craft was carried down the river by the current and hit one of the main pillars of the Jacques Cartier bridge. The driver, a French Canadian, was able to manoeuvre the damaged craft onto the river bank and the passengers were then able to get out with dry feet. However the craft was out of action for over a month and with the repairs, it cost us a great deal of money.

A further blow came when the Road Traffic Authority saw it being re-fuelled on shore at the maintenance base. This led ultimately to an assessment which concluded that the hovercraft was a commercial vehicle and therefore subject to fuel tax which just about took all our profit.

When the exhibition closed six months later the Canadian Government gave us a small contract to ship one craft to Churchill on the coast of Hudson Bay for an assessment of its capabilities in ice and snow.   Tony Smith, our Operations Manager, went up there to supervise and drive in January 1968 for two months and it proved to be most satisfactory, considering the local conditions with temperatures down to -43° F (75° of frost), and in wind speeds of up to 35 knots. The Neoprene (synthetic rubber) skirts were found to be more than adequate in the cold, as were the Ni-cad batteries but Tony had found it difficult to navigate in the conditions there as he had no electronic guide marks or radar to go by. By 8 March 1968 when he was due to return to England, he had operated the craft for 134 hours.

In the meantime another very unusual charter had been granted to us. An expedition wished to visit the South American Indians in the heart of the forests of the North part of Brazil. Sponsored by the Geographical Magazine, the aim was to test the feasibility of using the hovercraft for expedition purposes under rigourous conditions while providing a team of geographers with facilities for research in the little-visited regions of Amazonas. A party of 20 people, doctors, scientists, photographers and journalists was organised and we prepared a hovercraft for the journey from Manaus (a thousand miles up the Amazon), on the confluence of the Amazon and the River Rio Negro, over the height of land to the River Orinoco in Venezuela and on to Trinidad. By a freak of nature a canal of shallow water lies between the two main rivers. Fuel dumps were laid down at strategic points by boat and helicopter and they set forth on 11 April 1968 under the control of our overseas manager, Graham Clarke who had joined the company in 1967. He was an ex-Naval fighter pilot having fought in the Korean War.

Details of this unique expedition have been described elsewhere; it was a remarkable feat and the hovercraft proved to be reliable in very difficult conditions. The hovercraft was a comparatively new form of transport and Graham Clarke was being asked to take it 2,000 nautical miles over waters previously not disturbed by anything more sophisticated than an outboard motor! It was an arduous journey during which they encountered many obstacles but, in spite of great hardships by all members of the party, they duly arrived at the Caribbean on 7 May 1968, but not without incident.

There was an ugly moment for Graham when going down the

Orinoco River. They encountered the Maipure and Saniarapo rapids above Port Ayachuo where they realised that they were more like a waterfall. The Venezuelan Airforce provided a helicopter for an aerial survey from Isla Raton, an island just before the start of the rapids, in order to find the best route through the huge rocks. Graham thought it might be possible to navigate through but it would be highly dangerous and as it was not possible to go back to Manaus by the route that they had come as the territory was possibly hostile with Indians and the fuel dumps had been used up, he decided he had to 'go for it'. In order to reduce the risk to non-essential personnel and also to lighten the craft, Captain Clarke disembarked his passengers who travelled to Puerto Ayacucho via a rough road. The photographs of the rapids with the hovercraft emerging rather like a rubber ball from an area of boiling water, give some idea of his skill in navigating such a nightmare trip without damage. If the engine had been swamped it would have ended in disaster and I am sure his passengers were thankful when he pulled in at Puerto Ayacucho.

On arriving safely at Trinidad the British Hovercraft Corporation, from whom Hoverwork had chartered the craft, took it over, under their ownership, as they had decided to use the craft for a demonstration tour of a hovercraft's versatility in the major cities of the East Coast of the South American continent. Hoverwork provided a driver and BHC used their own engineers. The craft was carried on the deck of a ship and was off-loaded in Rio de Janeiro, Santos Montevideo and Buenos Aries.

Back in England the scientists were analysing their specimens of the food and medicines that they had collected from the natives and in due course gave lectures. Graham Clarke was invited to attend a lecture at the National Geographical Society in London about their journey from the Amazon to the Caribbean, one which had never been accomplished before by water, except possibly by canoe. The lecture was very well attended and Graham received well deserved congratulations as well as being presented with the Mrs Patrick Ness award for Geographical Exploration.

Another unusual charter took place in 1972 when Hoverwork surveyed the delta of the Mackenzie River on the Arctic Coast of Canada in the Northwest Territories, the land of the Eskimos. The SRN6 was to be used to make a seismographic survey of the coastal waters in that area. The largest oil field in the North American continent lay in Alaska at Prudoe Bay, 100 miles to the west of the

Canadian Border, its production being piped across Alaska to the Pacific port of Valdez.

Our craft was shipped to St John's, Nova Scotia, there to be loaded on a flat car to be transported by train to Hay River on the Great Slave Lake, a distance of about 4,000 miles. This relatively new railway line to Hay River had been built to transport heavy mining equipment to the huge area of potentially rich minerals in the far north.

From Hay River the hovercraft was driven over the rapids at the western end of the Great Slave Lake near Fort Providence on the headwater of the Mackenzie River to the Arctic, a journey of 1000 miles to Shingle Point. The nearest town was Inuvic, a recently built settlement for the tribe of that name, and sixty miles away. Although Inuvic had facilities for maintaining the craft for operating, either in the brief summer where the coastal sea was clear of ice or in the extreme cold of winter, all craft servicing was carried out at the base camp.

When the craft was reassembled and ready to start the survey, the Canadian authorities intervened by delaying the start of operations as it was the breeding area for whales and they did not want them disturbed. This meant that, in spite of the short season of open sea with the Barrier iced 10 miles off shore, the programme had to wait. However, once the amphibious qualities of the hovercraft had been explained, the operation went ahead without undue delay.

The government was very compassionate in considering the natural environment of both people and animals in the far north. Even in 1930 when I had been flying mail to the Arctic we had helped to establish a base a 100 miles west of the delta for a herd of reindeer due to arrive from Siberia. This herd was to provide food and transport for the Indian and Eskimo tribe whose Caribou stocks had become depleted. The Eskimos are now, 50 years on, very well provided for with doctors, houses and most of the comforts of civilisation but whether they are happier than in the past when they lived off seals and in igloos, is debatable. Their old nomadic culture, crude as it was, did not include alcohol, drugs and crime.

Canada's north has an abundance of minerals from gold at Yellowknife, uranium at Great Bear Lake, nickel at Churchill, Hudson Bay and oil at Northern Alberta but these are all inhospitable areas of extreme cold and isolation and virtually uninhabited land. The rivers all flow towards the Arctic Ocean where navigation by ship is virtually impossible but where amphibious hovercraft can offer transport in winter and summer; during the periods of freeze-up and break-up they must surely find a role.

While the South American and Canadian charters were going on the search for oil elsewhere continued as shown briefly in Appendix A. This work really provided a major supplement to our bread and butter revenue from the Hovertravel passenger service on the Solent. Many of these overseas charters made great calls on the men involved although they all went voluntarily. In many cases it involved considerable risk due to the nature of the locality but also physically, in that it meant carrying explosive charges used in seismographic search. It was tough work, often carried out in extreme heat or cold, but they were determined to show and prove what hovercraft could do and they were the pioneers in a new industry. I admired them greatly and their pioneering spirit.

Every trip abroad had its own story of hardship and courage but, although I had encouraged them to keep a diary with a view to publication, they were far too busy working and stories of their adventures have rarely been told. I am writing this 20 years after the events partly from memory but aided by those concerned, both drivers and engineers. They were true British pioneers with all the right spirit, courage and determination to show that our belief in the future of hovercraft was correct. It was not money that motivated them; they were all doing their duty and can look back on these events with pride.

The first accident we had occurred while making a survey in the Gulf. One explosive charge failed to go off and after searching for it without success, another shot was released resulting in a big explosion which damaged the stern of the craft extensively, in particular the propeller and transmission. Unbeknown to us the first charge had been trapped under the rear skirt, the second charge setting it off. In a second accident which occurred later, the explosion fractured the fuel tank and a fire ensued. Our Chief Engineer, Mr Wilkinson, who was on board, kicked other charges overboard but the whole craft was already engulfed in fire, killing him and ten others including several Arab labourers who had come from Aden.

In the first accident a technical investigation found that the craft structure had survived the underwater explosion and in the second, fire had caused its ultimate destruction. As a result of these two accidents the Navy took note of the protective effects of the air cushion on the structure.

An Egyptian SRN6 Hovercraft whose crew were under training

from Hoverwork personnel had a lethal accident off the Egyptian coast in the Mediterranean when a Liberian Tanker became stranded in the shallow water. Having passed the vessel on several occasions they decided one day to stop on the sandy beach and take some fresh supplies to the crew of the tanker but as the Captain stepped out with the prospective present he was shot and died instantly.

It was a very sad case as the driver, Mr Browning, was on his way home from Australia to see his pregnant wife and had stopped in Egypt to relieve the existing Hoverwork personnel. He had been driving one of our craft in Queensland which had been providing a travelling doctor service with the Aboriginals in the outlying Islands off the north coast of Queensland but unfortunately the operation had been withdrawn following some disagreement between the Provincial and Federal Government.

Apart from the overseas operations, we had several contracts around our own coast. One was to help establish an artificial Island in the middle of the Wash. Ham Dredging had been contracted to build a small Island there as a trial for a proposed sea wall which would form part of a very large reservoir of fresh water. The idea was for the Island to be tested as to erosion and strength as part of the feasibility study of the entire operation. Our job was to shuttle to and fro from the mainland at all states of the tide with men and supplies. This was a case of a hovercraft saving the company time and money.

Seismographic surveys were also made off the coast of Norfolk seeking a further extension of the existing Leaman Bank Field for British Gas. Much later, in 1976, we surveyed a large area of the Blackpool coast as far as Morecombe Bay which now produces a large proportion of the country's demand for gas in the industrial area of north west England. When the price of oil fell in the 1980's the requirement for seismic surveys, understandably, diminished to practically nil.

As craft became older we found a useful employment for them in hydrographic surveying on the north coast of Holland and the mouth of the River Rhine, both of which are dotted with many shifting sandbars and channels. Hovercraft, equipped with the latest hydrographic electronic measuring gear, could run a plot of the various channels thus ensuring the safety of a large number of big ships in this area where the main channel may have shifted. We supplied two of our SRN6s to a Belgian company which undertook this work.

In 1971 we helped a very unusual expedition on an uninhabited

Lord Mountbatten, Governor of the Isle of Wight, about to perform the opening ceremony of the Hovertravel route, accompanied by Mr and Mrs Robertson and Mr Desmond Norman

Sir Christopher Cockerell, inventor of the hovercraft, with Mr John Britten of Britten Norman Aircraft Co.

Vosper Thornycroft VTI en route to Sweden

Mr Peter Atkinson escorts the 2,000,000 passenger to Ryde

AP-188 en route - Portsmouth to Ryde, 1992

Canada, Hudson Bay, 1967. Tony Smith during trials in the Arctic.
A frozen tree snaps off

Amazon to Carribean expedition. Graham Clarke shoots the Maipures
rapids on Orinoco River, Venezuela

SRN6 Flatop, Hoverwork conversion. Loading a bulldozer for Hopen Island

Ducted SRN6 Hovertravel conversion for quieter running

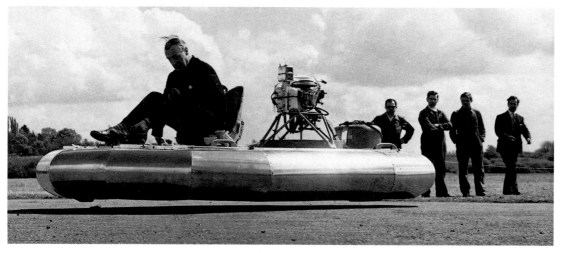

Skimmer, 1961. Demonstration at Redhill Aerodrome for BBC and College of Aeronautical Engineering

Skimmer II, 1962. Testing at home

Pindair Skima at Stokes Bay Solent

Pindair Skima at the Royal Festival Beach in London.
Note Russian hydrofoil in the background

Griffon 2000 TDX demonstrations in Hong Kong.
Destined for Yankze River in China

Three Griffon 1000 TD for oil industry support in China. Griffon office and workshop

Griffon 2000 TD at Calshot for five craft demonstration on Southampton water.
Dr Gifford with six engineers

Griffon 2000 TDX. Four craft for Royal Marines at Lock Long. Exercise for NATO 1994

Griffon 1000 TD at sea off Castle Point, Cowes

Griffon 1000 TD on River Lea clearing debris

Island, Hopen, between the north of Norway and Spitzbergen which had no jetty or landing facilities as it is largely ice-bound. After the first world war the League of Nations granted a mandate for the area to the Norwegians who decided to look for oil there. Being located in the Barents Sea, an area which the Russians dominated during the cold war, the operation presented rather a delicate situation.

The object of the expedition was to sink an exploratory oil well. The company which organised the operation was Belgian, the oil company was Norwegian, Norske Fina, and the icebreaker was Norwegian while the drillers were American. We supplied the hovercraft and crew to take the party and equipment ashore after blasting a slipway through a fringe of ice stranded on the shore. It was a big undertaking for us as, apart from the oil rig itself and the pipes, they had to establish a base with diesel generators, heavy lifting gear and living accommodation for the men. The proposal was for the rig and pipes, together with a bulldozer, to be put ashore in the early spring, the drilling carried out, and then everything to be out by the onset of the following winter.

In fact all went according to plan and the well was duly drilled but during this operation a Russian trawler took up a position a mile or so away and watched. They were obviously observing how far the drill went down and they could achieve this by simply counting the number of pipes that were sunk into the ground. I only heard recently that one day two Russian women geologists became marooned on the Island when the weather suddenly deteriorated. Our party offered them shelter for the night in our rather rudimentary living accommodation, ie. a shed. The following day our hovercraft Captain, Richard Drew, offered to take them out to their trawler which he did. On preparing to leave the trawler the Captain offered him a drink, in fact he insisted on it, and Richard found himself being pressed to have several more. The return journey was a happy one and the navigation back to the base was a little erratic to say the least! Whether the incident was a contrived one, we will never know.

When the drilling operation had been completed and tidied up the departure date was later than had been planned and with winter advancing and the increasing cold, the engine of the hovercraft refused to start. It would not fire up on the diesel oil as it was not vaporising properly so in desperation they tried squirting petrol round the intake with the result that the turbine burnt out. We immediately flew a spare engine out to Tromso in the northern most part of Norway and chartered an ice-breaker to take the engine to the hovercraft.

Somehow our engineers had rigged some shelter and in the oncoming winter darkness and cold, managed to get the new engine installed and working. This is known as working under difficult conditions and they have my full admiration, achieving almost the impossible so that all the men and our hovercraft returned to the ice-breaker safely.

CHAPTER XXI

An Era Ends

Having surveyed the north and west coasts of Saudi Arabia in 1974 to 1976, we then moved to Abu Dhabi in 1977 by which time the new legislation for British Hovercraft was in force. The annual inspection for the renewal of our safety certificate had to be made and as our SRN6 was in Abu Dhabi, the Civil Aviation inspector who was based there, carried out the necessary requirements. He was accustomed to clearing the Concorde which operated the air service from the United Kingdom and when it came to our SRN6 he was surprised to find it was looking somewhat scruffy after two years in the desert and the salty waters of the Gulf. Although aesthetically it did not look good compared to Concorde, he did eventually pass it as a safe vehicle.

By coincidence 1981/82 were spent on another seismic survey in Iraq on the very large Lake Habbaniya near the River Euphrates where, in the fresh water and also sheltered waters of the lake, we found that our maintenance costs halved and the aluminium hull was completely free of any sign of corrosion. The skirt will normally last for about 600 or 700 hours which at a cruising speed of 28 knots is about 18,000 to 20,000 miles, not very different from the tyres of the motor car. The rubber and nylon based segments wear more quickly around the bow and the stern of the craft but when the tips of the skirt segments are badly worn they can be patched with staples and glue rather like re-treading a car tyre. As each SRN6 skirt has 110 fingers fitted, which last the 600 or 700 hours, the rubber required to replace these makes them an extremely expensive commodity.

In a slightly different role we helped in a tidal land survey of the Maplin Sands near Southend which was War Office Property and had been used for testing guns and shells since the days of canon-balls. This area was under consideration for use as a fourth airport for London and we provided an on-call ferry service for the men stationed on a drilling barge located on the large tidal mudflats. This area of 40 foot deep mud and sand was not easily accessible and our hovercraft service speeded up the whole operation which saved the contractor costs.

About that time the government informed us that, in future, we would have to pay VAT on fuel. I felt that the imposition was not justified because the legislation on hovercraft specifically stated that they were not ships nor were they aircraft. Up to that time we had been eligible for a refund of tax under the Coastal Shipping Act while our rival, the government company Seaspeed, using Italian hydrofoils between Cowes and Southampton, were free of tax. Finally, after seeing the Minister Geoffrey Howe they gave us an exemption.

By 1980, with the seismographic work diminishing due to the big drop in the price of crude oil, and our ageing SRN6 craft, the Hoverwork company's workload was moving back to the passenger service on the Solent, our main source of revenue which had increased steadily through the years. The larger passenger craft, the AP188, which we had been considering for some time was given the go ahead with our own capital reserves together with the 50% backing of the National Research Development Corporation (NRDC). The first AP188 four engined craft had been designed, and detailed drawings prepared, by Mr Peter Winter of Air Vehicles Limited for 80 passengers but in all the following production craft the hull was stretched to increase the number of passengers to 100. Larger 525 hp turbo charged Deutz engines were installed and the whole programme moved ahead.

We then received a big shock when NRDC suddenly withdrew their financial help while insisting on the finishing and fitting out of our already completed hull being carried out by BHC employees in our workshops at Bembridge Harbour!

I was angry over this episode, making a very strong protest to Mr Stanton Jones, the Managing Director of BHC at East Cowes, especially as he had previously refused to build a bigger craft for Hovertravel with diesel engines and had even written to say that it was completely impractical because of the engines' extra weight.

In fact Mr Jones was a good friend of mine but the whole affair in my opinion was over the patent of the segmented skirt about which there had been some dispute. Hovercraft Development Limited, a subsidiary of NRDC, which had Christopher Cockerell as its Chairman, eventually retained one patent while BHC held a slightly different one. Meanwhile I was so angry at the withdrawal of funding I decided to resign as Chairman of Hovertravel, giving the excuse of moving aside to make room for a younger man. After I had left, the Managing Director of Hovertravel, Christopher Bland came to an agreement with BHC concerning the various disputes which satisfied all parties concerned.

The AP188 programme was in fact eventually part-funded with a very expensive loan by NRDC's successor, British Technology Group. The only good thing about the loan was that if the AP188 failed, the money did not have to be repaid.

By this time I was 72 years of age and did genuinely feel that it was time to bring in some younger men. The job of running the companies of Hovertravel and Hoverwork no longer required a person with technical expertise, rather they needed someone with business acumen which was not my strong point. Upon my resignation Dr Gifford took over as Chairman temporarily followed by Christopher Bland, the present Chairman, who has led the company from strength to strength.

In 1978 I had been asked to join the Banks Committee which had been formed to advise and make suggestions for the possible future development and promotion of the hovercraft industry and the best course to take. We had about six meetings in the Millbank Tower in London and Mr Banks, who was a retired director of BP, was the Chairman. He had gathered a number of people from the practical side of the hovercraft industry with a civil servant taking notes.

All seemed to be progressing well until it was brought to a halt shortly before the Department of Trade and Industry announced that it was stopping all future development of hovercraft. Hovercraft Development Limited was to be disbanded and all future expenditure was withdrawn except for the paying off of current contracts. This was the government's policy (the terminal grant) or in other words, no more government money.

The new policy had little effect on Hovertravel or Hoverwork as they had not been receiving any money except for services rendered (eg. taking Margaret Thatcher for a trip at Brighton) but the policy of terminal grants applied also to any possible interest by the Armed Services, the Coastguard, the Police or any other section of the community which in any way was dependent on government money. This meant that the door had been closed to many possible contracts.

The finances of Hovertravel improved dramatically after taking delivery of the first AP188 and progressed even further when the company sold one of the AP188s from the Solent route to an American company, Bell now called Textron Marine. They initially leased it for the US Navy as a training craft for the drivers of a new big hover landing craft which could carry a 60 ton tank. After a while they decided to purchase it and two years later Hovertravel sold them a second craft from the Solent route which greatly enhanced the company's asset value and also enabled them to buy a used AP188 from Australia and for themselves to build another new craft at Bembridge. At the time of writing this book, 1994, Hovertravel's passenger service, still using the AP188, has carried well in excess of 13 million passengers across the Solent.

In 1990 Hoverwork Ltd received an order from Westland, our old friends, for us to build an AP188 for a Russian company, The Northern Shipping Company, for a craft to be used in the White Sea. The sea there is partly free of ice due to the Gulf Stream but the mainland cities of Murmansk, Archangel and other coastal towns, are icebound.

The building and fitting out was sub-contracted to Hoverwork by Westland who had negotiated the deal with Russia. The standard accommodation was altered to a 60 passenger craft with 8 bunks and a small cabin with a cafeteria type of galley. There were large heaters to deal with the cold and an auxiliary diesel generating unit fitted to meet the extra demand for electrical power. The Captain's bridge was equipped with very extensive electronic equipment for navigation and communication purposes.

Five Russian drivers, all merchant seamen, and five engineers were trained by Hovertravel and Hoverwork and the Russians also assisted our own men to build the craft at Hoverwork's yard at Bembridge Harbour. The new craft was to have been named by the Russian Ambassador at the Westland BHC works at East Cowes on 11 September 1991 but, following the Gorbachev resignation, he was suddenly recalled to Moscow and in his place, to everybody's surprise, they sent the young Russian beauty Queen! She made a short speech and the official party were taken on a trip to Osborne Bay. Before doing so I decided to make my first inspection of the newly built craft and while I was sitting in the driver's cabin the Russian Beauty Queen came in and we started talking. She told me that she had come to London the previous month in order to learn English and I took some photographs of her sitting at the controls. Over lunch at the Old Manor House Restaurant, part of the Osborne Estate, I found myself being sat next to her. Someone must have thought that as I was 84 years old she would be quite safe. To me she looked quite aristocratic, with high cheek bones and wearing a very smart French looking outfit.

Several years prior to my resignation as Chairman of Hovertravel, Dr Gifford and I had formed and registered a new company, Griffon Hovercraft Company, Griffon being a combination of our names Gifford and Robertson. Because of our involvement in Hovertravel and Hoverwork we had not activated the company but my departure provided the opportunity for us to do so and as my own convictions of the viability of hovercraft had never waivered, I transferred all my efforts to the new company.

CHAPTER XXII

Doing It Our Way

Ella and I had moved from the country to London in 1965 soon after our daughter, Jane's wedding. I had to do a great deal of travelling at that time and Ella was busy in her charitable work with the National Children's Adoption Association. Unfortunately she was knocked over by a wave while trying to rescue a young friend of Jane's from the sea at Aldeburgh and soon after developed very bad headaches. After seeing many doctors to no avail, she went to St Mary's Paddington where the specialist put her on an anti-coagulant, a new drug at the time, which helped her greatly. Afterwards she was in the hands of various doctors but from that time I always made a point of returning to our home in London at night. Meanwhile I had been having trouble with my eyes and was under the care of Moorfields Eye Hospital.

Even with these health problems, all was going well until the fire in our flat in 1969. Although we seemed to recover from having lost all our possessions, it must have given us a greater shock than we had realised because it seemed to become a turning point in our lives. The rebuilding of the flats was going to take over a year to complete so we decided to set up home in another flat about a mile away. It had been a year of frustration and strain which led Ella to smoke more until she began to develop signs of emphysema. Again she came to rely on doctors but she would not consider moving out of London. I had many commitments at this period of my life and I perhaps should have given them up to look after her. My resignation from Hovertravel made little difference to my home life as she encouraged me to keep active and of course I was starting up Griffon.

In 1982 the small hovercraft company Griffon Hovercraft Limited became more active as my partner, Dr Edwin Gifford, took over control and devoted more time to it. We began to manufacture smaller hovercraft in some buildings on Dr Gifford's own property near

Southampton, these new Griffon craft incorporating all our own ideas of low cost workboat type hovercraft.

The hulls were welded aluminium, the engine a diesel driving a wooden propeller in a duct, while the sidebodies folded upwards for transport by road or in a container as this enabled the craft to be carried to areas for overseas operations, a major factor. We had managed to finance the design and prototype out of our own resources, and we were fortunate in that the prototype performed well without any serious modification. At that point an American Company in the heavy transportation industry in the USA took a licence from us and bought the prototype. From then on all subsequent craft were sold on contract with a first pre-payment followed by subsequent stage payments, the normal method for marine craft.

The first Griffon was a six seater with a wooden hull built to fit inside a slightly enlarged standard Dunlop pneumatic dinghy to provide buoyancy, fitted with a 4.2 litre Jaguar petrol engine of 200 hp, driving a four bladed aircraft type wooden propeller in a duct. The transmission was by the standard Jaguar clutch, via an HTD Uniroyal toothed belt to a large diameter slow turning propeller. The lift fan was driven off the front end of the crankshaft via two Vee belts. Both the propeller and the skirt were designed by Bob Trillo, a professional consultant, whereas the hull structure and engine mountings were designed by Dr Gifford who was a Civil Engineer. My own contribution was concerned with the aerodynamics and transmission which, by incorporating a clutch, permitted the lift to be separated from the thrust.

The design of flexible skirts had advanced rapidly by this time but in an effort to avoid the cost both of royalties and construction, we unwisely specified a bag type skirt instead of the more recently patented segmented type. The original trials were carried out on Southampton Water but, although we were very pleased with the available thrust and quietness of the ducted propeller, the bag skirt, although it did plane, had far too much wetted surface which created drag. By modifying the skirt to the Hovercraft Development Limited's segmented type there was a great improvement in performance.

A feature which we had incorporated in the original design was the use of a vehicle type clutch on the engine. This permitted the main propeller drive to be disconnected using a normal car type foot pedal. Manoeuvring was exceptional as the craft could be hovered by speeding up the engine with the clutch disengaged to generate lift, and using short bursts of thrust by engaging the clutch and speeding up the propeller. By use of the clutch and rudders, the craft could then be trimmed bow-down, pivoted on its bow skirt and turned on the ground within its own length.

Development proceeded satisfactorily but neither of us could devote the time to consider production at that time so we entered into an agreement with Mr Pinder who, with his own company Pindair, was already producing a four seater craft. We agreed to re-design the hull of our model as an all aluminium structure and to help with the installation of another engine, the American Chevrolet V-8 of about 200 hp. This craft was put into production under the name of Skima II. A number of modifications were incorporated over the years, the most important one being the skirt shift system which had been developed, using a Skima II, by HDL who still held the patents of the skirts. This skirt shift enabled both the lateral and fore and aft trim to be altered by using two electrical winches to alter the geometry of the skirt and so moving the centre of lift in relation to the centre of gravity. For practical purposes and simplicity only the lateral skirt shift was used in production but this gave marked improvement in control of the craft, for example in cross winds. It also improved manoeuvrability by deliberately heeling the craft and using the extra drag on the lower side to turn in the required direction.

The latest development in skirt design has led to reduced skirt drag, improvement in wave capability and a reduction of power to lift, thus saving fuel consumption while improving efficiency both in performance and costs of operation.

The Skima II was manufactured at Gosport where the shallow tidal area, part of the main Portsmouth Harbour, was an excellent location for hovercraft demonstration as there was a big area of mud and marsh with a background of many laid up warships moored in the main deep water channel. The craft remained in production for some years, about 20 being sold world-wide before the factory closed.

Dr Gifford and I were still very conscious of the cost of operating hovercraft and also of the advantages of diesel engines in marine applications as compared with petrol. We calculated that, with the knowledge that we had, it would be possible to build a hovercraft with a one ton payload carrying capacity using an air cooled diesel engine of 190 hp. Although much heavier than the equivalent petrol engine, the advantages of safety from fire, fuel economy and long life between overhauls, gave the use of diesel power a big advantage over any previous hovercraft.

The new Griffon 1000TD (Turbo Diesel) was designed to carry 1,000 kilograms or 10 people. Instead of the previous pneumatic sidebodies or fenders which had proved a nuisance in hot tropical countries as they had to be re-inflated daily, it had watertight aluminium sidebodies, which could be folded upwards for transport on the road. These provided a very convenient deck space for the crew and for carrying unusually bulky external loads, such as oil drill pipes or survey equipment. It could be containerised for shipping and conformed to the legal requirements for trailing on the road.

The Deutz Type BF913 air-cooled diesel engine which was turbo-charged and inter-cooled, is a well proved engine mass-produced for coaches and trucks. It was mounted together with the pylon, propeller and duct as a unit which could be assembled on a bench and dropped into position. Considerable thought went into the design of the engine cover to give good accessibility and at the same time to seal the machinery space from salt spray by providing adequate filtration for both engine cooling air and air for combustion.

Apart from the repositioning of one of the fan bearings to eliminate some vibration, the trials went very well and careful measurement of the performances showed that the maximum speed in calm water was 34 knots. At cruising power the fuel consumption was only four gallons per hour. The prototype was sold to our American Licensee, they passed it on to the Marine Police on Chesapeake Bay, who operated the craft for over two years. During this time they kept a very careful record of its operating costs, reliability and of spare parts used. They also made a thorough report on the suitability of the craft for police purposes which delighted us as they commented most favourably on its performance and its valuable use.

The next three craft went to China and were based at the mouth of the Yellow River where oil had been discovered. The frequent flooding and particularly glutinous alluvial mud there, makes the area inaccessible to all normal forms of transport but our Griffons proved very effective when operated by the Chinese drivers, sometimes carrying 20 people, the overflow sitting on the deck. As the lift is generated by the pressure of air in the cushion, any load is very evenly distributed over the whole structure and, therefore, unlike aircraft, overloading is not a very serious matter, although when coming to rest the craft must be lowered gently onto its landing pads.

The Chinese drivers showed great skill in handling these craft as they are naturally good boat handlers. One at least had never even seen a motor car while another bought his craft back to base with a broken rudder cable; he had steered it back by shifting his crew from side to side!

From the performance of the Griffon 1000TD it was clear that there was adequate power to drive a larger craft. This stretched version was called the 1500TD carrying 15 persons or 15,000 kilo. The smaller craft had a fabric hood which could be folded to leave the crew space open but the aluminium hull itself was the main load-bearing structure. This gave us the opportunity of providing a variety of different fibreglass cabin tops to meet customers requirements for protecting the passengers. The driver's wheelhouse also had a bulkhead with a lockable door for security against theft when parked, while the main cabin was in two sections so that it could be supplied either as a complete cabin with a door on either side, or with half cabin for a crew forward and the other half open for convenience as a workboat.

In 1988 a Griffon 1500TD, a stretched version, manufactured in the United States by our licensee, Hoversystems Incorporated, was supplied to the ITT Antarctic Service in McMurdo Sound. The craft proved most successful completing 350 hours in the first six months even operating in winds up to 40 knots. The scientific community were delighted as the speed and range of the hovercraft, together with its manoeuvrability in the prevailing conditions of ice and snow, proved a very satisfactory new tool for their purposes apart from providing a warm cabin in which to change. They also considered it would make a good vehicle for logistic purposes on the central Polar Plateau. Their only complaint was that over a big hummock of snow and ice it would run away down the slope out of full control. The fitting of a variable pitch reversing propeller overcame this snag.

CHAPTER XXIII

Stretching The Market

One of our original intentions in designing the engine and propeller as a unit was to enable us to use two similar units side by side to double the thrust and lift capacity for a larger craft, without having to redesign the machinery. An opportunity arose in 1985 when our American friends wanted a larger passenger craft to operate at the Expo '86 Exhibition in Vancouver. Because we already had the engine/propeller units in production, we were able, at short notice, to offer a twin engined craft capable of carrying 32 passengers. Carrying visitors from the heart of the City, the terminal of the historic Canadian Pacific Railway Terminal, round Stanley Point, to False Creek where the main Exhibition was being built, it offered a beautiful scenic alternative to the car or train. The Exhibition was to open on 1 May 1986 but following a series of delays we did not get the go ahead for the building of the craft until April 1985 which left us little time to complete the detail design and build it. It also had to undergo acceptance trials, and UK and Canadian certification for use as a public transport vehicle, had to be obtained. It then had to be shipped to the Pacific via the Panama Canal and San Francisco where it gave demonstrations before carrying on to its destination.

The Griffon 2500TD, as it was called, arrived in time for the first scheduled trip but leaving little opportunity to train the Canadian personnel who were to operate the craft. The Griffon Company was essentially a manufacturing business but inevitably we found ourselves involved in providing drivers, engineers or training to ensure that our customers fully understood both its capabilities and correct maintenance. We had originally recommended two craft in order to maintain a regular timetable but with the time restriction the production of two craft was not possible so, as a compensation, we gave them as much support as we could considering they were 6,000 miles away. I went out to Vancouver, staying with John McGrath who was in charge of the Canadian Coastguard Hovercraft Operation located at the airport there and who had been using SRN6s for some years.

Shortly after starting the service it became apparent that the skirt segments were tearing and wearing out very quickly. The available spares were soon used up and although we flew out further supplies, there was obviously something very wrong and we eventually found out that the batch of the synthetic rubber coated nylon supplied by the factory, was faulty. Unfortunately our company's reputation and goodwill was badly damaged as our other operators in Australia and Panama had suffered the same problem. The factory were unable to give us a satisfactory explanation for the fault but I believe that one of the chemical agents in the material had been left out.

Having finally overcome the skirt trouble the Canadians were unfortunate in having an engine failure when the crank shaft failed, almost unheard of in a Deutz air-cooled diesel. The faulty engine was flown back to Germany for critical examination by the company.

In Vancouver a large floating raft of logs was constructed as the authorities would not allow the craft to use their VIP pier at the CPR terminal. It was easy for the passengers to embark and disembark as the hovercraft climbed onto the raft at one end and re-launched from the other, thereby demonstrating the fact that it was amphibious. The route itself did not allow it to display this feature as there were no sand bars although the local waters had many loose floating logs which caused damage to the propellers of conventional craft. One of the Griffon 2500's main features was the excellent visibility from the cabin enabling the passengers to get an exceptional view of this beautiful City and Stanley Park with its enormous trees, as well as a view of Grouse Mountain with its cap of snow in the distance.

On entering False Creek from English Bay there are two bridges and from there to the Exhibition there was a speed restriction of 6 knots which was strictly enforced to prevent wash. For the hovercraft this restriction was an unnecessary disadvantage as it does not generate wash or waves when planing over 15 knots but at 6 knots it is below 'hump' speed causing the skirts to create drag. For the last one and a quarter miles to the jetty the craft was, therefore, shown at its worst taking a great deal of time to complete this stretch. Under these conditions it was unable to demonstrate its ability to travel fast in confined waters without making a wash or causing spray, its main features. The only advantage of this slow journey was that the passengers were able to gauge the extent of the huge Exhibition site and the position of the various Halls.

We had hoped, of course, that this venture would generate hovercraft sales and to this end I enthusiastically conducted a large party of Japanese around the main shipping harbour. Unfortunately they were only interested in the facilities for docking and ship repairs for their own ships, taking only a passing interest in our craft. On the first day of the Exhibition we took out the Governor of the Province of British Columbia and his party. He was very interested in the craft asking many questions, but when he disembarked at the Exhibition there was no reception party or media gathered to greet his arrival. Apparently there had been some disagreement in the media about the expense of the Exhibition which was being cold-shouldered; other people's politics are a mystery to strangers!

Before leaving Canada and being transported to Philadelphia where the American licensee had its factory, the hovercraft had completed 1,250 hours. The operation and experience were invaluable to us and back in England, despite the problems we had encountered, there were many enquiries for twin-engined passenger carrying craft.

The economics of passenger transport always call for craft which can carry more people so we set about designing a bigger 40 to 50 passenger twin but it is not easy to see ahead in a market which had not yet been established. Every operator's requirements are different and in order to keep control of the ultimate cost, we decided to concentrate on two basic hull sizes, each with the option of being stretched using the same basic design. So far as power is concerned Deutz offered a range of powers from the 190 hp in the original Griffon 1000TD to 625 hp, a V-12. With this range of hulls and engines we could offer a carrying capacity from one to five tons or, alternatively, 40 to 50 passengers in reasonable comfort, fully comparable with Economy Class on the airlines, but with leg room! Most overseas operators require heating, air conditioning, a galley and a WC as well as extensive electronics for navigation.

The first two twin-engined craft went to Thailand for a passenger service between a hotel on an outlying island and the mainland. The Thais were familiar with hovercraft as the previous year we had supplied three Griffon 1500TDs to their Royal Navy for patrol work intercepting smugglers and also for transport of VIPs. A number of the smaller craft were also sold to Pakistan for water conservancy work and pollution problems while a contractor working for the

Panama Canal Company used one to transport the big ship pilots between the ships and their base; the railway was unreliable and the roads were at the mercy of bandits.

At home in the United Kingdom we obtained a contract to carry commuters across the Thames from the old Greenwich Gasworks to the Isle of Dogs, a three minute shuttle service for Reuters' employees who lived south of the Thames. We employed two Thames watermen to operate our Griffon 2000TD on this work and after the disaster of the sinking of the pleasure boat, Marchioness, we were asked to lend the craft, with the operators, to the Thames Police.

Our contractor gave permission and the hovercraft was used in the unpleasant duty of collecting some of the bodies which had become stranded on muddy banks of the river on the receding tides; both the police and the Port of London Authority were glad to have the craft at their disposal.

Another unusual contract was to ferry men across Morecombe Bay to a big dredger engaged in digging a trench for British Gas, in preparation for laying a new pipeline to Northern Ireland. Another job was to survey at close quarters every jetty on both banks of the River Thames as, under recent legislation, the jetties had become the owner's responsibility. This work brought the small hovercraft's versatility to the notice of the Port of London's Authority who looked on our activity with some interest. There is no speed limit on the Thames but wherever repair or construction work is going on, especially if there is a diver involved, there is a speed restriction of six knots. They noticed, however, that at 20 to 25 knots the hovercraft made virtually no wash or wave, a great asset, although the noise level is higher. We did not receive any complaints but we decided to run at reduced speed when the noise level is insignificant. In the early days of Hovercraft the noise generated the largest number of complaints but great progress has been made since those early days.

The Swedish Coastguard ordered one of our craft for use as a Patrol Craft for the Baltic which, in the northern part, freezes in winter. After a year's operation they ordered two more as they recognised the value in stopping illegal immigrants from Russia entering Sweden, intercepting drug runners, ice patrols and checking buoys which could become shifted by ice. They also used them for rescue work particularly during the period when the ice begins to break up.

During 1988 we had been approached by an old friend, Michael Cole, an ex-Royal Air Force Officer, to charter a 2000TD craft for an ambitious expedition to China, sponsored by Sir Edward Heath, the former Prime Minister, who had visited and made friends in Beijing. Mike Cole had raised a sum of money and the enthusiasm of a medical team from Loughborough College, to take a UNICEF vaccination programme to Tibet on the upper reaches of the Yangtze River near the source of the river, a height of 15,000 feet.

We set about preparing a craft for the expedition together with a smaller craft, a River Rover. The craft were financed by Neste, the oil and chemical company from Finland while the other party to the contract was the Chinese Academy of Science which was of course a vital part of the expedition as it required a great deal of organisation. The standard engine in the Griffon 2000TD was the Deutz supercharged turbo-diesel with an inter-cooler but we had it modified by Deutz to give it as much power as possible at 15,000 feet.

After giving a demonstration to authorities in Hong Kong the party, following unbelievably complex negotiations, finally left in March 1990. After a long journey by train and truck through the mountains, with many adventures en route, they reached their base camp at Denke on the upper reaches where there were a number of rapids to be surmounted. Part of the medical programme had to be dropped as the last possible date for departure was approaching, but they did reach the source of the river or, at least, as far as the ice would permit, a height of 4,800 metres (16,000 feet) a world height record for hovercraft.

During 1992 the Norwegians asked Griffon Hovercraft Limited to demonstrate a 2000TD on the Arctic ice cap, north of Spitzbergen. They were interested in the ability of the craft to climb out of the sea onto the floating ice up a ledge of about 18 inches, which was in fact, about the hover height of the craft.

On the way to the trial and in company with an ice-breaker, our craft proved faster through the broken sea ice than the ice-breaker simply because it avoided the big chunks by going round them!

A detailed description of the expedition to China was recorded in a book written by Dick Bell, 'To The Source Of The Yangtze' published in 1991 by Hodder and Stourton Ltd but I have mentioned this and the other contracts in order to portray the versatility of the hovercraft.

The marketing of hovercraft has been a problem. Few people appreciate what an amphibious craft is, frequently being confused with hydrofoils, sidewalls, SES (Surface Effect Ships) and catamarans. None of these of course can operate over shallow or debris laden water as they depend on water propellers for propulsion. A large number of enquiries are concerned with routes which do not require a hovercraft's amphibious capability which must be exploited to justify the cost compared with a conventional boat. There are in fact limitless special applications in which convenience, a reduction of time saving labour costs, access to inaccessible areas or rescue purposes, come into play. With the helicopter, which is extremely expensive to operate, a very large market now exists after a slow start; the same could well develop in the hovercraft's specialised role.

While all these developments were taking place I had had to slow up while the next generation took over. John Gifford, Dr Gifford's son, and his contemporaries ran the company very competently with his father, now an OBE, taking a supervisory role. Gradually they learned the complicated business side of tendering, sales, export permits, letters of credit, etc. which in a larger company, there would be special departments. Our Overseas Sales Manager, Mr Graham Gifford, (no relation), previously employed by Vosper Thornycroft, travelled extensively and knew the right people as he had set up his own sales company of fast marine vehicles.

Ever since the government had decided not to invest in hovercraft or their development, there has been little scope for hovercraft companies to gain contracts from the armed services in the UK but to our surprise, in 1993, the Ministry of Defence ordered four Griffon 2000, suitably modified for use by the Royal Marines. This was a great moment for us and the company made every effort to meet their target date. We had given demonstrations in the past to the Royal Marines and nothing had come of them but I can think of a number of military operations in which they could be invaluable, the Normandy landing for instance or mine counter-measures; a hovercraft can cross landmines without detonating the charge. Present hovercraft have many advantages for underwater work as I know from our experience while engaged in seismographic surveys.

The course of my life had changed completely when my wife, Ella, died of emphysema in 1985. After 48 years of being happily married and with my daughter and her family living in Wales, I felt very lost. I had no reason to live in London, or any particular area, so I finally decided to move to Bembridge on the Isle of Wight where my niece lived and where I knew a few people. I have made many mistakes in life but that decision was not one of them for the local people were very friendly and they made me feel more than welcome.

I bought my own little house in the village which gave me the opportunity to relax with peace of mind and as my sight was still deteriorating, it was helpful to be close to the shops and a bus stop as I could no longer drive a car. My life had always been an active one and it was difficult to settle down to living alone. The Griffon factory was nearly two hours travelling time away but I kept in touch with my partners and, since retiring from Griffon in 1992, they have always invited me to see each new design.

With time on my hands and a reasonably good memory the thought of sitting down and writing about the early days of hovercraft and the other strange marine craft in which I had been involved, kept my mind active. I also took lessons in painting which gave me a weekly routine and a chance to meet many interesting people as well as learning something about the artistic world which was entirely new to me.

Early this year, 1994, I was invited by Griffon to attend the acceptance trials of the four craft ordered by the Royal Marines. I was proud and pleased to be part of that day as in a way it proved that my confidence in the hovercraft has not been misplaced.

Date	Location	Client	Type of Operation	Type of Terrain
1969	Holland - The Waddenzee	Petroland	Seismic Survey	Shallow water, tidal area with large sandbanks at low water
1969/70	Abu Dhabi	ADOC	Seismic Survey	Very shallow water with coral reefs
1970	Bahrain	BAPCO	Gravity Survey	Shallow water with coral reefs
1970	Holland - The Waddenzee	NAM	Seismic Survey	Shallow water, tidal area with large sandbanks at low water
1970	Tunisia - Sfax	CFP	Seismic Survey	Very shallow water
1970	Algiers	CNAN	Passengers	Transport from port to Fair site incl. half a mile of special road
1971	Saudi Arabia - Red Sea	Auxerap	Seismic Survey	Very shallow water with coral reefs
1971	Holland - The Waddenzee	Petroland	Seismic Survey	Shallow water, tidal area with large sandbanks at low water
1971	Holland - Dollard Bay	Deutag Drilling	Servicing Drilling Rig	Shallow water, tidal area. Three miles of sand at low water
1971	Arctic Circle	Norske Fina	Logistics	Pack ice over shallow water - plateau of rock with depths from 0.5 to 6 feet
1971	England - North Sea - Haisbro & Leaman Banks	Phillips	Seismic Survey	Very shallow water, moving sandbanks with tidal streams. Wrecks - rendering unsafe & impractical to use boats
1971/72	Tunisia - Sfax	EGEP	Seismic Survey	Shallow water & shore-line landwork
1972	Canada - Mackenzie Delta	Pan Canadian	Seismic Survey	Shallow water & shore-line land work
1972	UK - The Wash	Wimpeys	Servicing Barge Operation	Shallow water, tidal area with large sandbanks at low water
1973	UK - Maplin Sands	Wimpeys	Servicing Barge Operation	Shallow water, tidal area with large sandbanks at low water
1974	Sweden/Finland	Waxholms	Passengers	Ice & Ice Water Operation
1974/76	Saudi Arabia	ARAMCO	Seismic Survey	Shallow water, coral reefs & sandbanks
1975	Holland - Emshaven	NPC	Servicing Barges	Shallow water & sand
1975	UK - The Wash	Ham Dredging	Servicing Reservoir	Shallow water, tidal area with sandbanks
1975	Australia - Torres Strait	Dept of Aboriginal Affairs	Hospital Service	Shallow water & coral reef
1976	UK - N.West Coast	British Gas	Seismic Survey	Shallow water, tidal area
1976	Algiers	CNAN	Passengers	Transport from port to Fair site
1977/79 1980	Abu Dhabi	ADOC	Seismic Survey	Very shallow water & coral reefs
1981/82	Iraq	INOC	Seismic Survey	Inland lakes in part mudbanks & small reeds

Date	Location	Client	Type of Operation	Type of Terrain
1984	Philadelphia U.S.A. Chesapeake Bay	Hake Incorporated	Marine Police Patrol & Rescue	Inland waters. Patrol Chesapeake Bay
1984	China Yellow River	Texas Instruments	Service of oil rigs Seismic survey	Mud & marsh
1985	Pakistan	Crown Agents	Reservoir survey (Hydrographic)	Marsh & dykes
1988	Pakistan Rann of Kutch	Crown Agents	Civil engineering survey	Marsh & mud
1989 - 1991	River Thames Greenwich	Rosehaugh Construction	Transport of passengers	Shallow banks of river
1987	Canada Vancouver	Hake Incorporated	Ferry to Exhibition	Harbour to open sea to exhibition. Waters with floating logs
1992	Bombay India	New India Business House	Commuters city to residential area	Partly sheltered waters
1989 - 1991	Thames River	Thames Water Co	Survey & photography of banks	Shallow water
1991	Sweden North Baltic Arctic	Swedish Coastguard	Patrol. Navigation Buoys. Ice. Immigrants.	Open sea & snow covered land. Broken Ice. Icefields
1993	Scotland	Ham Dredging	Carrying out crew changes for dredger	Shallow water Open water
1992	Various operations on sea & land	M.O.D.	Royal Marines	All types of amphibious uses
1992	Norway Spitzbergen	Norwegian Scientific Research	Hovercraft trials on ice cap Arctic.	Snow. Broken ice. Arctic Sea. Ice cap
1990	Thailand	Royal Thai Navy	Communications Patrol. Immigration	Shallow river
1991	Thailand	Thai General Transporation	Tourist transport	Hotel to mainland